BRIAN BRAITHWAITE

Women's Magazines

The First 300 Years

PETER OWEN

London

PETER OWEN PUBLISHERS
73 Kenway Road London SW5 0RE

This edition first published in Great Britain 1995
© Brian Braithwaite 1995

A catalogue record for this book is available
from the British Library

ISBN 0–7206–0936–4

Printed in Great Britain by Biddles of Guildford
and King's Lynn

Contents

Introduction

I have been actively involved in the world of women's magazines during the past thirty years (and other magazines for even longer), and the huge weight and variety of titles that have for so long been directed at the female sex have always fascinated me. From the society and fashion journals of Victorian days, through the cheap and cheerful twopenny titles of the pre-war years to the elegant, glossy superstar magazines of today, women have been bombarded with a plethora of products written and produced expressly for them. Whether they be housewives, career women, débutantes, sportswomen, brides, teenagers or dowagers, they have represented that important figure known as the reader.

Women's magazines can inspire passionate loyalty from their readers and titles can publish for decades. But tastes vary along with current fashions and trends, and these factors have combined to create some spectacular and expensive flops. To the casual male reader women's magazines can appear strikingly homogeneous within their different categories, but each title enjoys devoted readers. But most magazines, like their readers, eventually fade away and make room for fresh entrants with new ideas.

There are over eighty magazines on the market that are directly, or obliquely, aimed at women. The editorial standards are necessarily high for them to survive in the cut-throat commercial world in which they have to compete. Advertising and readers have to be fought for and kept. The magazines are under constant scrutiny with their circulation figures audited every six months by the Audit Bureau of Circulations and their readerships regularly dissected by the National Readership

Survey. The reader's social class, age, sex, and the magazine's similarity to other titles are all examined under the microscope by the advertising agencies and media buying shops. And even when a magazine passes the statistical and tabulated analysis by these commercial gurus there is still the abstruse and intangible ingredient known as 'editorial atmosphere': the tone and voice of the magazine. Does it have the ambience and environment which will appeal effectively to both the reader and the advertiser? Sheer statistics are not enough, but they certainly help to set the advertising rate in context with the market.

As the lives, status and careers of women have changed, so have their magazines, striving to attract the readers' interest and loyalty. This book attempts to record the history of the women's magazines, the comings and goings of titles over the years. Some have been seminal, many less so, but they have all sought their fortunes on the bookstalls. The book is, of necessity, a whirlwind tour across the magazine canvas, often with passing snapshots but occasionally pausing to examine the more influential titles which have changed the industry's perceptions and directions.

I have endeavoured to give a flavour of the style and content of some of the older magazines with extracts from the editorial and sometimes readers' letters. Whenever possible I have allowed the editors of newly launched titles to speak for themselves, to delineate their magazines' ambitions and to define the readers they hope to attract. Sometimes these editorials are doom-laden as we read them with the smug benefit of hindsight, but their cheerful and self-confident aspirations make brave and assured reading.

I have to acknowledge my debt to Cynthia White for her remarkably researched book *Women's Magazines 1693–1968* (Michael Joseph), a considerable help in recording Victorian and Edwardian publishing. Other books that have given useful material along the way are *Frontiers of Privilege* by Francis Wyndham (Collins), *Advertising in Victorian England* by Diana and Geoffrey Hindley (Wayland), *The Lady's Realm* (Arrow Books), *Oscar Wilde* by Richard Ellmann (Hamish Hamilton), *Women in Wartime* by Jane Waller and Michael Vaughan-Rees (Optima) and *Home & Country* (Ebury Press.) I would also like to acknowledge help from Michael Bird and particularly Joan Barrell, my co-author on our two books on *The Business of Women's Magazines*.

I must also thank the publishers of all the magazines from which I have quoted whether they (the magazines!) are living or dead.

One
1693–1911

'Not another new women's magazine!'

One can understand the exclamation. Almost every week sees a new title attempting to edge its way on to bookstalls already brimming with magazines directed at the female sex. Women's magazines are a phenomenon. Some titles come and go at an alarming rate, others have been with us since the twenties or longer. That amorphous mass known as women readers are loyal and fickle, young and old, intelligent and dull, working and leisured, rich and poor. The publishing industry invests impressive chunks of money into finding new products, defending old ones, researching markets, hiring and firing editors, improving production values and generally trying to reflect the way women live. Each up-and-coming generation of readers has to be excited with the shock of the new. They will probably eschew the magazines that their big sisters read and certainly the ones that their mothers did. The classic magazines, mostly home-based, rumble on for years, while all around them there is the constant and insistent search for ideas and products to titillate the palate and to exploit the lives that women lead.

Mere men have never been the beneficiaries of such a superabundance of magazines. 'Men's magazines' have come to mean rather lascivious products featuring the female anatomy, to be found on the newsagent's top shelf. But men are, in fact, voracious readers of magazines – witness the broad spectrum of hobby and motoring titles, and sports magazines that are male-orientated. There are the new 'style' titles for men but no general feature mass magazines specifically directed at the sex. There is no male equivalent of *Woman* or *Woman's Own*, *Bella* or *Best*, *Options* or

Marie Claire, *Cosmopolitan* or *She*. My attempt at *Cosmo Man* back in the seventies was not a success. It's *women* who adore magazines and have done so increasingly over the past hundred years.

We have to whizz all the way back to 1693 to discover what was seemingly the first-ever women's magazine. The *Ladies Mercury* was launched by a London bookseller, John Dunton. It claimed to provide answers to all 'the most nice and curious questions concerning love, marriage, behaviour, dress and humour of the female sex, whether virgins, wives or widows' – thus setting a pattern that would be emulated and developed through the centuries. The style was uninhibited, frank and prurient, not unlike many of the titles for younger readers today.

The eighteenth century saw a crop of almanacs, or diaries, directed towards the female population. These were annual publications, the fore-runners of the modern pocket diary. They featured a calendar and pub-lished a wealth of relevant information on all sorts of topics deemed to be of interest to their audience. Most famous and endurable was the *Ladies' Diary*, which first appeared in 1704 and was published annually until 1841 when it merged into the *Gentleman's Diary*. The *Diary* was egalitarian in its editorial coverage – Ladies, Waiting Women and Servants, Mothers, Virgins were all encompassed by the annual issue of information about cookery, family life, love and marriage.

As well as the annual diaries there were the more frequently published journals. *The Tatler*, although a general magazine, directed much of its editorial towards the female sex and the improvement of ladies. *Tatler* is Britain's oldest surviving magazine. Its two-year publishing break in the 1960s (when it was transformed into *London Life*) cannot take its lon-gevity record away from it. Other noted titles of the period were *Free-thinker* and *The Visitor*, both determinedly interested in improving the minds and manners of their female readers. *The Ladies' Journal* espoused the cause of women's education, and in 1728 Mrs Penelope Prattle ed-ited the *The Parrot*, more devoted to improving the morals and virtue of her readers than to entertaining them.

The word 'magazine' was coined by Edward Cave, a printer, when he published his *Gentleman's Magazine* in 1731. His design and formula were swiftly imitated, particularly by *The Lady's Magazine*. In 1747 came *The Lady's Weekly Magazine*, edited by Mrs Penelope Pry, which tended towards the pompous and rather dry comments on current affairs. It lasted but three years before the *Ladies' Magazine*, published by the pleasantly named Jasper Goodwill, was launched at twopence a copy. A fortnightly consisting of seventeen pages, the title was almost what we have come to know as a part-work, as it was intended to be a complete volume at the end of a year's publishing. It set out to entertain and amuse with an editorial mix of love, history, science, news and wit. There were riddles and puzzles, play reviews and even a history course. But a central plank of editorial policy was the detailed record of crimes and punishments, with sensational and grisly contributions from eye-witnesses. The life of the *Ladies' Magazine* was ephemeral as it died with its publisher in 1753 – only four years after its birth.

The middle of the century saw a quartet of recorded titles: *The Lady's Curiosity* in 1752, followed by *The Old Maid*, *The Young Lady* and *The Lady's Museum*. *The Old Maid*, a title that would not endear itself to today's single women was a haphazard affair editorially, and lasted a mere six months. *The Young Lady* achieved only seven weeks. *The Lady's Museum* fared better, an intellectual review with poetry, essays and translations from the French. Another *Lady's Magazine* appeared in 1770, and it was rewarded with a lifespan of seventy-seven years. It was of literary bent as was its imitator, *The Lady's Monthly Museum*, which followed a few years later.

Now that the magazine format was beginning to take shape the titles appeared thick and fast. The most notable was *La Belle Assemblée* in 1806. This was professionally produced – no alliterative pen names for the editors, and was particularly quick to seize on the popular device of publishing readers' letters. The tone was educational, geared towards improvement of the mind. *The Monthly Museum* carried advice for the young and was, perhaps, the first title to feature an agony aunt. This was 'The Old Woman', particularly good on matrimonial, or would-be matrimonial, advice. *The Female Preceptor* in 1813 aimed to produce a literary work for ladies with essays, poetry, fashion, astronomy and other information.

The first recorded merger of magazines took place in 1832 when *The Lady's Magazine*, *The Lady's Monthly Museum* and *La Belle Assemblée* joined forces, although they continued to publish separately with identical contents. They all ceased publication in 1847, bringing to a close the period of Georgian influence. The magazine business was now ready for the less elegant but more rumbustious Victorian years.

But the first recorded title of note in the reign of Victoria was the relaunched *La Belle Assemblée*, imaginatively re-titled *The New Monthly Belle Assemblée*. Morally upstanding, the new magazine featured plenty of fiction (in which virtue always triumphed) and reviews of plays and books. It carried a series on English churches, and touched on rather mundane social issues. *The Ladies' Cabinet* carried on in the same moral and pious vein, while the *The Lady's Newspaper* and *Pictorial Times* in 1847 went for a higher intellectual capacity in its readers. All the titles assumed that their readers were affluent and middle class – the accent was on the word 'Lady' in so many titles.

But the industry underwent a sea change in 1852. Prior to that date, the upmarket magazines customarily cost one shilling, a cover price that put them out of reach of many women. A young man of twenty-nine called Samuel Beeton, who was married to Isabella – a lady of notable culinary skills – published *The Englishwoman's Domestic Magazine* at the startling and attractive price of twopence a copy. He opened up the vast, untapped readership of the middle-class woman, an area hitherto neglected by the other publishers. It is not an exaggeration to say that Beeton invented the 'popular' women's magazine, which was developed over the next hundred years with such skill and energy by his successors.

Beeton dedicated *The Englishwoman's Domestic Magazine* to 'the improvement of the intellect, the cultivation of the morals and the cherishing of domestic management'. Isabella contributed weekly notes on cookery and fashion. She travelled twice a year to Paris to report on the spring and autumn collections, a mandatory duty carried out by fashion editors ever since. Beeton even invented the paper dress pattern and ran competitions. For your twopence he threw in gardening notes, fiction, literary criticism, articles on household pets and personal hygiene. Inevitably, he had his advice page under the heading 'Cupid's Advice Bag'. This concentrated predominantly on courtship and marriage problems with a rather moral rectitude in its answers to correspondents.

The Englishwoman's Domestic Magazine was a hit. In four years the circulation had mushroomed to 37,000 copies, reaching a record 50,000 by 1860. In that year Beeton relaunched the title with better quality paper and coloured fashion engravings. The price went to sixpence, but the magazine was firmly established and ahead of the field. In that relaunch year came *The Lady's Review*, reacting to the new mood for women's rights which was sweeping the country with radical demands for new laws. In 1846, *The Female's Friend* had attempted to espouse this cause through the medium, but it fizzled out in months. *The Lady's Review* also found the feminist atmosphere a tough one and foundered within the year. By contrast, *The Ladies' Treasury* in 1858 was back to the traditional values, with fiction, fashion, needlework and absorbing pastimes for the young Victorian woman who had no need to go out to work or to get involved in feminist politics. This title ran for thirty-seven years, outliving a whole crop of militant, activist magazines.

Woman's World was a name to be used several times over the next century. The first magazine to be so called was overtly political and eschewed the fripperies of fashion in favour of The Movement. The title changed in 1869 to *The Kettledrum*, subtitled *The Woman's Signal for Action*. The editorial line was somewhat softened to include art and literature but even so the mixture was too heady and the magazine closed within the year.

In 1872 came *The Ladies*, a sixpenny monthly, which described itself as a journal of Court, Fashion and Society. Its death came within the year and, again, its demise was due to its mild but definite feminist leanings. Although fashion was its principal theme, it ventured too far into the sensitive areas of politics and social privilege.

Samuel Beeton, prospering with his *Englishwoman's Domestic Magazine*, strengthened the establishment's stand against social militancy with his publication of *The Queen* in 1861. Here were no feminist politics, no revolutionary and discomforting thoughts for its overtly affluent readership. His declared policy was unambivalent:

> When we write for women we write for the home. We shall offend
> very few when we say that women have neither the heart nor the
> head for abstract political speculation, which as for our own liberties,
> or our own political principles, they may safely be left to men...
> therefore our survey of foreign affairs and of politics generally will be
> recorded in a few notes.

Queen Victoria graciously gave permission for her name to be used, a devastating ploy to any would-be competitors and, at sixpence a copy, *The Queen, An Illustrated Journal and Review* was launched into the world of society. The editorial concerns were high fashion and high society. The doings of the Court were of prime interest to the readership of lords and ladies, gentlewomen, chaperones and débutantes. This was the Golden Age for the moneyed and the aristocratic, and *The Queen* was unashamedly British, snobbish and contemporary. It was to go through numerous editorial phases until 1970, when it was merged with *Harper's Bazaar* to become *Harpers & Queen*.

The women's movement even generated its own magazine backlash in 1869 when a sixpenny monthly awkwardly entitled *The Girl of the Period Miscellany*, appeared as a light-hearted protest against the cause for women's rights. Edited by 'Miss Echo', it championed the desires of young women who preferred a more insouciant and frivolous life to the serious suffrage cause. With its cartoons and irreverent commentary it was a cheerful, satirical magazine, despite its clumsy title.

But the movement continued to want magazines to push their views and opinions. One of the most practical was *Woman's Gazette*, which in 1875 advertised employment opportunities for women. We have all read those Victorian novels where the governess or tutor is desperate for work, even at the low rates of pay then offered by the richest employers, so *Women's Gazette* must have answered a real need. With thousands of women on the labour market, and no labour exchanges or other government agencies, the magazine must have seemed an inspiration. But the title attracted little support and was soon changed to *Work & Leisure* – perhaps something of a cop-out, but it continued to give employment advice and lightened the load with entertaining features and competitions. It carried on until it sank in 1893.

As Victoria's reign continued, with its great social problems as well as its unbounded affluence and aggressive international security, the middle classes continued to expand and flourish. The growth of industrialization brought new opportunities to thousands of young women who deserted the traditional role of domestic service and found clerical jobs and work in the bustling distribution and retail trades. The shortage of servants meant that the middle classes, in particular, were often confronted with their own domestic chores. This brought a demand for household hints and information, recipes, dressmaking tips and other domestic necessities. This was fertile ground for a new wave of magazines to exploit and service a huge new market. Two such initiatives were launched in 1876: *Myra's Journal of Dress and Fashion* and the famous *Weldon's Ladies' Journal*, destined to enjoy a long and successful life until its final demise in 1963, when it disappeared into *Homes & Gardens*.

The last twenty years of Victoria's reign coincided with a great energy and expansion in the world of women's publishing. During that period, forty-eight new titles came on to the market. With the 1870 Education Act, elementary education took a giant stride forward and later acts extended the scope of education to all classes. More people could read and thirsted for knowledge and entertainment in print and train travel gave them more time to read. A series of tax changes also considerably helped to stoke the magazine fire. Stamp duty was abolished in 1855, advertising tax in 1858, and paper duty in 1861. The way was open for cheaper and less sophisticated publications with family appeal at low cover prices. Typical titles were *Dickens' Household Words*, *Mirror of Literature, Amusement and Instruction* and *The Family Friend*.

In 1842, Mr Mudie established his lending library in Oxford Street and W.H. Smith started to extend his chain of station bookstalls, closely allied to the startling advance of the railway system. The first W.H. Smith railway bookstall opened on Euston Station on 1 November 1848. There were to be disputes with the railway companies in 1905, but the following year W.H. Smith had established 144 shops on stations or station approaches. There can be little doubt that the rapid and comprehensive build-up of the railway bookstall networks must have been of considerable importance to the development of the popular women's magazines of the time.

Mr Mudie's Circulating Library was flourishing in the middle of the century. Originally based in Upper King Street (now Southampton Row), the business was moved in the 1850s to New Oxford Street. Mudie's operated on an unprecedented scale, exercising great influence on the popular literature of the day. It was his practice to place large advance orders for books of which he approved. He also ran famous literary re-unions in the hall of the New Oxford Street headquarters, which were attended by prominent literary figures. When Mudie's finally went into liquidation in 1936, there were 140 branches. There is no doubt that Mudie's was a considerable factor in developing the public taste for reading.

W.H. Smith had begun in 1792 with the distribution of newspapers, magazines and other periodicals. By 1855 Smith's had already become the largest wholesaler and retail news agency in England and Wales. They also began their famous library in 1858, which went far beyond the scope of Mr Mudie due to their country-wide network of railway bookstalls. The 1830s saw the beginnings of another historic bookshop chain when John Menzies set up in business as a retail bookseller in Princes Street, Edinburgh. He soon expanded into the wholesale trade and the handling of newspapers and periodicals. He ventured into publishing on his own account, with Scottish guide books and a famous work on the costumes of the clans. In 1857 he linked up with the Scottish Central Railway by taking the station bookstalls at Perth, Stirling and Bridge of Allan. The network rapidly expanded. The first women's magazine handled by Menzies was *People's Friend*, published in 1869 by the Thomson family at Dundee.

The other extensive railway bookstall chain was Wyman's, since absorbed into the John Menzies empire.

With the popular explosion of magazines and a whole new literate generation eager to read them, the technological advances in the paper-making and printing trades were of crucial importance. Paper had been an expensive commodity, reliant on a supply of rags. The solution came from Sweden, where sulphate was successfully produced from wood pulp. This answered the need for the huge quantities of cheaper grade paper. Printing also took a great leap forward with the introduction of new rotary presses, which could print significant quantities at high speed. Hand in hand with the acceleration of the presses came the development of the typesetting process, which had been traditionally manual. In 1889, the introduction of Linotype allowed the typesetter to cast whole lines of type mechanically. Photographic reproduction of line drawings, and later photographs by the half-tone process, were the other printing innovations.

It was inevitable that the new readership, and all the excitement of the technical developments would throw up new publishing giants to exploit and indulge these profitable new markets. Three names in particular shone out in the pioneering new industry: Alfred Harmsworth (later Lord Northcliffe), George Newnes and Arthur Pearson. These names were to echo down the corridors of publishing power for nearly a century.

Alfred Harmsworth had started writing at school by editing the *Henley House School Magazine*. His first professional job was as assistant editor on *Youth*, later writing social paragraphs for *Vanity Fair* (the old Spry Journal) and short stories for a boys' paper called *Young Folks*. He sold articles to *Titbits* (owned and edited by George Newnes) and there met Arthur Pearson, who was destined to be his greatest professional rival. In 1888 Harmsworth founded the weekly publication *Answers to Correspondents* – later shortened to *Answers* – which he handed over the following year to his brother Harold to run and edit. The Harmsworth empire eventually numbered more than seventy weekly and monthly publications.

Answers achieved national fame and notoriety when in 1889 it offered a lucky reader £1 a week for life for the closest estimate of bullion held in the Bank of England on December 4th of that year. The competition drew an amazing, record-breaking 718,218 entries.

Harmsworth's genius was his brilliant insight into the sort of reading matter that would appeal to the new mass market of working-class readers. He gave them romance, excitement, entertainment and a smattering of general knowledge. Perhaps today he would have gone into television and produced soaps. Certainly before the advent of the cinema his popular press provided the diversions and entertainment for this eager audience. Harmsworth had plenty of competition, not least from Arthur Pearson, in launching titles for the popular end of the market. Pearson's *Home Notes* in 1894 was one of the outstanding successes in women's monthlies.

George Newnes had started *Titbits* in 1881 after reading about a runaway train in Manchester. He decided that a magazine full of interesting 'tit-bits' about odd stories and interesting facts would be a success. He opened a vegetarian restaurant to provide himself with the necessary finance. The magazine sold over 200,000 copies within a couple of years and survived right up to the 1980s.

Both Harmsworth and Pearson produced bright and cheerful weeklies for the new markets during a period that also saw the launch of the popular *Family Herald Supplement*, featuring weekly serials about the high life 'above stairs'; a monthly for the more curious and educated, called *The Strand Magazine* (later to publish the Sherlock Holmes stories), and *The Idler*, edited by Jerome K. Jerome. By 1889, younger readers were treated to an illustrated penny weekly called *Ally Sloper's Half Holiday*, the famous halfpenny *Comic Cuts* and a girls' title, *Forget-Me-Not*.

As the circulations of all the exciting new magazines and journals soared so, of course, did the costs of printing, paper and distribution. The modest cover prices generally failed to meet these costs, just as they do today, so the Victorian publisher was forced to turn to the advertiser to subsidize publication and to provide the profits. The repeal of advertisement duties opened the door to the huge opportunities afforded by the plethora of new popular magazines, and such opportunities were not lost on the enterprising businessman. Earlier in the century, the more up-market magazines had been most reluctant to be involved with such vulgar commercialism, but they gradually became willing to accept a limited number of advertisements, usually confined to the covers. The new publishers, however, exhibited no squeamishness about carrying advertising and openly courted it. One can imagine that the business was quite uncontrolled with the advent of the Audit Bureau of Circulations still some forty years off. Advertisements were no longer relegated to the covers but spread through the magazines to face editorial pages. The speed and variety of the new launches must have been bewildering to the advertisers, particularly as one can imagine the exaggerated claims about circulations and readerships proffered by the publishers.

The year 1885 saw the launch of *The Lady*, the very same weekly publication that is still with us today. *The Lady* is, in fact, the oldest surviving women's magazine in Britain. It was the brainchild of Thomas Gibson Bowles, who designed it to appeal to 'women of education and to provide entertainment without vulgarity and information without dullness'. Bowles, a man of many roles, including participation in the 1870 seige of Paris, had launched *Vanity Fair* in 1868 on a capital of £200, with immense success. He spotted 'a gap in the market' for a magazine for the intelligent woman. His editorial credo was spelt out in the first issue:

> *The Lady* is presented to the public with the confidence that a
> journal of its kind will commend itself to those for whom it is
> intended. Our object is, and constantly will be, to cover the whole
> field of womanly actions, to ascertain what kind of information it is
> that women of education most need, and to provide them with that
> precise information. Whether it is the more serious business of
> woman's life, or in those matters apparently more trivial, yet scarcely
> less important, which relate to its adornment and beautification, we
> shall seek to furnish them with all such useful and worthy aid as can
> possibly be given in the pages of a weekly journal. Our purpose is to
> make *The Lady* at once a valuable friend and a delightful companion;
> and to this purpose we shall not restrict ourselves to the old paths,
> but shall seek the aid of novelty in matter, in methods, and in
> treatment whenever it appears best calculated to fulfil our purpose.

The Lady's editorial contents were mixed, to include social events and fashion as well as the customary competitions. After a lacklustre start, the editorship was taken over by Rita Shell, who had been governess to Bowles's four children. Shell, who was to remain editor until 1925, introduced small advertisements. The magazine flourished from that point, and to this day, *The Lady* is famous for its pages of classified advertising, full of nannies and holiday cottages. Even after all these years the title is still in private hands, never having been seduced by the financial blandishments of the big publishing houses. It may seem rather irreverent to say, but the deliberately staid editorial pages constitute a distinctive pattern, which could easily have been destroyed by any major publishing company's streamlining attentions. In short, *The Lady* readers like their magazine exactly as it is, and some 80,000 of them still purchase it every week.

A crop of other new magazines were launched around the last decade of

the century, many of which were to enjoy reasonably long lives. The hearth
and home were well to the fore with *Home Notes* (1894–1957), *Home Chat*
(1895–1958) and *Home Companion* (1897–1956). *The Ladies' Field* (1898–
1928), *The Ladies' Review* (1892–1908), *The Lady's Realm* (1896–1915)
and *Woman's Life* (1896–1934) were other entrants, with varied life cycles.
Further titles at this time were *The Young Gentlewoman* (1892), *Madame*
(1895), *Princess* (1890), *Schoolmistress* (1881), *Woman* (1890), *Young Ladies' Job* and *Lady Cyclist* (1895). The reader will already have observed a
certain repetition of titles as the magazines came and went over the years.
The names Lady, Woman, Girl, Home, World, Realm, Life, Friend, Letter,
Journal, Wife, Companion and Mother were perpetually thrown into the
melting pot in the early days of women's magazines, and throughout the
twentieth century they have been used repeatedly in various permutations.
The latter years of the century have witnessed an imaginative use of totally
new magazine names, to avoid the clichés of the old ones: *Bella*, *Best*,
Take a Break, *Nova*, *Cosmopolitan*, *Prima*, *Big*!, *More*! and *Hello*! are
examples that spring to mind.

We have to linger over the launch of another magazine at this time.
The Lady's World, subtitled *A Magazine of Fashion and Society*, was
started in 1886 by the book publisher Cassell. The publishers asked
Oscar Wilde, then aged thirty-one and before his sensational successes
and sensations, to edit the journal. Wilde was seeking a livelihood and
took the offer seriously. As he wrote to Wemyss Reid of Cassell:

> I have read very carefully the numbers of the *Lady's World* you
> kindly sent me, and would be very happy to join with you in the
> work of editing and to some extent reconstituting it. It seems to me
> that at present it is too feminine, and not sufficiently womanly. No
> one appreciates more fully than I do the value and importance of
> Dress, in its relation to good tastes and good health: indeed the
> subject is one which I have constantly lectured on before institutes
> and societies of various kinds, but it seems to me that the field of
> the *mundus muliebris*, the field of mere millinery and trimmings, is to
> some extent already occupied by such papers as the *Queen* and the
> *Lady's Pictorial*, and that we should take a wider range as well as a
> high standpoint, and deal not merely with what women wear, but with
> what they think, and what they feel.

Wilde planned to concentrate on articles on the education of women and to relegate the fashion element to the rear of each issue. He accepted a salary of £6 a week and set about recruiting society women to contribute. His impertinence in asking Queen Victoria to contribute a poem was indignantly rejected. He also concerned himself with the title of the magazine, and urged the directors:

> The present name of the magazine has a certain taint of vulgarity
> about it, that will always militate against the success of the new
> issue, and is also extremely misleading. It is quite applicable to the
> magazine in its present state; it will not be applicable to a magazine
> that aims at being the organ of women of intellect, culture, and
> position.

His desire to change the title succeeded, and *Woman's World* appeared in November 1887 with Wilde's name on the front cover. Wilde displayed a nonchalant attitude to the onerous task of editorship over the twenty or more issues that he was in charge of, finally handing the magazine over to another Cassell editor in 1889 after a period of falling circulation.

Woman's World has over the years been an obvious and much employed choice for a magazine title and Odhams Press selected the name in 1903 for their magazine, which ran until 1958. The 1903 version was probably the forerunner of the modern woman's magazine, with an emphasis on the housewife and the younger working girl. Household affairs were its main thrust, accompanied by the vogue for rather lurid fiction. Carlton Publishing resurrected the name once more in 1977, a venture that was to die in 1990.

Certainly the domestic life, motherhood and the home preoccupied magazine publishers during the Victorian period. The titles speak for themselves: *Home Notes, Home Chat, Home Companion, Hearth & Home, Woman at Home, Ladies' Home Journal, Housewife, The Mother's Companion* – all dedicated to the new middle-class who had to get through their lives without servants, or probably only one or two. They were, in today's vernacular, 'service magazines'. Two of them, *Home Notes* and *Home Chat*, were so successful in fulfilling their function that they survived for sixty years, finally succumbing to the magazine economics of the 1950s. Pearson's had launched *Home Notes* in 1894, closely followed by Harmsworth, never to be outdone or outgunned, with *Home Chat* in 1895. They cost a modest penny but were full of practical domestic advice for the home-loving housewife. This was publishing for suburbia with unpatronizing and entertaining editorial. They were soon selling nearly 200,000 copies each by the turn of the century, a not insubstantial circulation given the massive competition of the day. They were probably the precursors of the twentieth-century popular weeklies like *Woman* and *Woman's Own*, and later the supermarket service monthlies.

One would like to think that Mrs Pooter, at The Laurels in Holloway, was an avid reader of at least one of the domestic periodicals. With her house-proud standards, her social climbing ambitions and her six-roomed, semi-detached house, she was right in the demographic mould of the new magazines. But, alas, there is no reference in *The Diary of a Nobody* to any women's magazine. In fact, the only title mentioned is *The Bicycle News* – and even that was borrowed from the neighbour Mr Cummings, making Mr Pooter one of the earliest recorded pass-on readers.

The growth of women's magazines in the remarkable period of Victorian England has to be seen in the context of the wide-ranging social changes. Wages had risen in real terms for the average worker by some sixty per cent over forty years. Job mobility, due to the railways, had greatly increased the opportunities for employment. The Metropolitan Railway was extended as far as Chesham by 1889. And the bicycle was the new rage – there were nearly five thousand manufacturers of bicycles in 1887. Again, these machines increased job mobility but also afforded personal transport to tens of thousands for leisure and pleasure. The consumer was born and suddenly the Victorians had a feel for marketing. There were two million members of the Co-operative Retail Society, giving easy access to new goods for the working classes. The middle classes had their department stores like Peter Robinson, John Lewis and Mr John Barker's new emporium in Kensington. New products tumbled out of the factories by the thousand, many of them directed towards women.

And, of course, women in their domestic environment, or 'new women' were the target for much advertising and marketing. A glance through Victorian advertising shows the ingenuity and skills of the commercial artist and copy-writer in reaching out to the new audiences of consumers. Such respectable journals as the *English Woman's Year Book* and the *English Illustrated Magazine* carried advertising for Southall's Sanitary Towels, not a subject for everyday conversation in the drawing-room, but treated with Victorian dignity in the advertisements. Beecham's saw the humour of exploiting the 'new woman' during the passionate women's liberation days of the 1880s with their advertisement of a betrousered, tie-wearing, cigarette-smoking woman declaring, 'Since taking Beecham's Pills I have become a New Woman! (Thousands can say the same which proves they are truly Worth a Guinea a Box!)' The soap manufacturers were soon in the pages of the magazines with Pears, Lever Brothers, Lux and Sunlight. Brooke & Co of King's Cross relied on their Monkey Brand, which not only promised Smiling Housewives, Clean Baths, Happy Husbands and Contented Servants but would clean, scour and scrub oil-cloths, bicycles, guns, swords and helmets.

Elliman's recommended their embrocation to lady cyclists for stiffness, aches, sprains and bruises. 'I will have it or I will have none' said a bloomered lady astride, followed by an elderly Edward VII look-alike on his three-wheeler. Eno's, for Health and Purity, were regular advertisers with ornamental inserts. Bovril and Colman's Mustard were ubiquitous in the magazines and on posters, not above portraying the Pope with a steaming mug of their product: 'Two infallible Powers'. Cadbury's Cocoa portrayed the Queen herself with their beverage and Princess Alexandra was pictured with her eponymous dentifrice. Cosmetic manufacturers were obvious advertisers in the women's press. M. Beetham of Cheltenham offered their glycerine and cucumber to 'Keep the Skin Cool' during the hottest weather: 'If applied after visiting Heated Apartments, Tennis Play-ing, Walking, Yachting, etc it will be found Delightfully Cooling and Re-freshing and will remove all Heat and Irritation.' Testimonials were common. Pear's used Mrs George Weldon in May 1897: 'I am fifty today but thanks to Pear's Soap my complexion is only seventeen.' Cherry Blossom, associated today with boot polish, were selling their perfume, toilet water and soap accompanied by a drawing of a nun. The slogan 'nun nicer' was inevitable.

Fashion advertising was the obvious draw for women's magazines. Corsets, bustles, millinery, knickerbockers, underwear and dresses decorated the pages. *The Queen* carried, appropriately, an advertisement for 'My Queen Vel-Vel – the only fabric which adapts itself to all the changes of fashion in all the newest art shades'. The latest fashions quickly spread to all classes, encouraged and exploited by the editorial and advertising in the magazines.

The younger sector of the market was not neglected during the new publishing boom. *Girl's Own Paper*, first published in 1880 and probably scoring as the first teenage magazine, began life as a weekly but moved to monthly frequency as the younger readers asked for a bigger magazine with more illustrations. Eschewing fashion in its early days, it soon introduced that vital element, particularly as the magazine became popular with the mothers of the readers. Another title for the adolescent was *The Young Woman*, aimed at a rather superior, educated readership.

It is possibly socially significant that the use of the word 'Lady' in titles began to give way more and more to 'Woman' at the turn of the century. Indeed, in 1890 came *Woman*, which was overtly middle-class, moving away from the society element of the 'Lady' magazines. *Woman's Health & Beauty* in 1902 had the explicit editorial aim of promulgating healthy living, physical culture and beauty. It ran for eighteen years under a male editor. In 1906 came *The Matron*, designed for the older woman, not the senior female figure in a hospital. *The Matron* was an antidote to all the publishing activity for young women. Eighty-seven years later there is still a publishing search for the older woman title amongst the glut of magazines for the woman in her twenties or younger. *The Matron* survived for ten years, disappearing during the Great War, with its editorial concentrating on fashion rather than child-care or more personal problems. No publisher at the end of this century seems to be satisfied that a magazine for the older woman is a goer, since women of a certain age hesitate to ask at the bookstall for a magazine with such ageist connotations. Further, publishers believe that a woman of sixty, say, will buy a magazine to reflect her interests (house, garden, fashion, etc.) rather than her age.

The year 1890 saw the launch of *Ladies' Home Journal*, which seemed to be a predecessor to *Good Housekeeping*. Indeed, *Good Housekeeping* appeared in the United Kingdom in 1922, one year before the death of the *Journal*. This 1890 magazine was rather sniffy about most of the new domesticated titles and took itself very seriously as the advocate of sensible home management and a reference guide to middle-class, responsible housekeeping.

Harmsworth was in his publishing heyday. His Periodical Publishing Company, later called the Amalgamated Press, was formed in 1891. His first contribution, a new weekly called *Forget-Me-Not*, was edited by Biddy Johnson, who went on to create a number of mass-market titles. The botanical title was a symbolic reference to purity and freshness. At one penny a copy, it became one of Harmsworth's most successful ventures, encouraging him to launch *Home Chat* in 1895 as an eyeball-to-eyeball rival to Pearson's *Home Notes*.

The turn of the century must have been an encouraging and stimulating time for the magazine publishers. Women were emerging as a political and social force – they were getting jobs, travelling, motoring, cycling, joining clubs for their hobbies and becoming avid readers of magazines. And the magazines were only too ready to respond to their thirst for information, education and entertainment. Publishers were beginning to see the financial advantages of targeting their titles to specific classifications in order to attract the advertisers. Magazines began to be directed positively towards the young, or the middle-aged, working girls, society women or housewives. The country itself may have been becoming more egalitarian, but the classes knew their places in society. The middle classes, probably springing from humbler origins, dissociated themselves from the working people, as society did from the middle classes.

The society journals were flourishing as well as the mass-market titles. *The Queen* was riding high and chortled about its younger readers:

> The girls of the day are fine girls, handsome girls, well grown and well developed; they have a splendid physique, they are strong and healthy and have good appetites and good digestions. They can dance into the small hours of the morning, night after night; they are good for any numbers of games of tennis; they can row a good stroke on the river, they can paddle a canoe, they can make up an eleven at cricket.

These Joan Hunter-Dunnes were, of course, the cosseted classes – their less affluent, working equivalents were out and about earning a living to improve their lot. But all of them were meat and drink to the magazine publishers after their weekly pennies or shillings.

The century turned. Victoria died and the halcyon days of the Edwardians began. The decade saw great wealth, sumptuous socializing for the rich and titled and the steady development of the lower and middle classes. A magazine for the more opulent and socially fortunate was *The Lady's Realm*. It was born in 1896 but sank during the First World War in 1915. In 1904 it was at the height of its success. Overtly snobbish, decorated with photograph after photograph of the aristocracy, it typically concerned itself with the protocol of entertaining Their Majesties the King and Queen in one's home if the royals 'signify their willingness to sojourn beneath the roof of any member of the British aristocracy. No greater honour or more signal proof of esteem and friendship can be accorded or received'.

The magazine liked to discuss burning issues of the day with such questions as 'Is Bridge Immoral?' They pooh-poohed the concept that women did not look attractive at the wheel of the Edwardian motor cars: 'Nobody can ever again possess the courage to revive the tradition, which should have been dead and buried years ago, that motoring destroys feminine attractions. Perhaps it was a libel invented by the comic papers'.

The magazine covered the London theatre season extensively and gave a rave review in 1905 to Mr Barrie's 'fantastic' *Peter Pan*. Cookery pages contained recipes for seven-course Edwardian dinners. But their *cause célèbre* in that year was a series of hard-hitting pieces on 'The Truth about Man' by 'A Spinster'. The author was a well-known novelist 'who prefers not to reveal her identity', and the series was a treatise for women on getting and handling their man, written with a trace of cynicism and perhaps a touch of gentile sensationalism. The series seemed to have generated no little heat amongst the readers and a monthly competition was run for their replies. One guinea was won by Mrs J.B. Hobmann of Chesterfield for her elegant riposte:

Although I am bound to admit that I am one of those unfortunate women who are not to be accounted an authority on the male sex, because married to one of them; still, by virtue of the time when I was also a 'Spinster' and a 'Free Lance' and looked at men from the outside with a magnifying glass, I may perhaps claim to give an opinion. Even now my 'duties', though they may not leave me time to take the extensive bird's-eye view of mankind taken by the writer in *The Lady's Realm*, provide me with ample opportunity to obtain a practical if not a 'scientific' insight into the masculine character.

I do not intend to make use of the inhuman methods of vivisection adopted by your correspondent in dividing and subdividing the species, nor do I think it possible to cram so varied a class into three or four little pigeon-holes; but, roughly speaking, one may safely say that there are Men's Men and Women's Men, and that it is only of the latter, as a rule, that spinsters have any experience. After a woman is married, if she is wise enough to encourage the visits of her husband's bachelor friends, she finds that there is a large proportion of men who carry with them, for perhaps the whole of their lives, that feeling of wholesome contempt for the feminine sex which is so freely and openly indulged in by the average schoolboy. It is in these men, that one finds the genuine attributes of their sex.

Good, honest, straightforward fellows, staunch friends or open
enemies – not over-conceited or super-sensitive themselves, and
expecting others to bear friendly criticism – genuine and generous,
what wonder that they are contemptuous and completely nonplussed
by the superficiality and unreality of feminine methods, or disdainful
of women's friendship, with its capriciousness, its little meannesses,
and its frequently insincere or diplomatic motives! Doubtless these
misogynists are included by the 'Spinster' in the class entitled 'The
World's Good Fellows,' for they certainly retain a great reverence for
their own ideal of Womanhood. But far from having no opinion of
themselves and remaining bachelors from motives of unworthiness, I
maintain that it is of women that they have no opinion, and in whom
they have no confidence; and until the sex realises that there must
be a great deal more 'Truth about Women' the 'Spinsters' will find
that their choice of husbands will still rest between the empty-headed
Male Flirt and the 'Mercenary Getter-On.'

Well worth the guinea prize!

A seminal launch came in 1910 when the Dundee publisher D.C. Thomson
brought out *My Weekly*, specifically for working-class women and still in
print today. The magazine helped to shape the traditional formula for popular
women's magazines – cookery, knitting, romantic fiction, dress-making,
child care, gossip and personal relationships. The editor aimed for her
own personal relationship with the reader, the 'one to one' so sought
after by her successors over the decades. The title said it all; the personal, possessive intimacy of that 'my' was the mood successfully achieved
over the next eighty years, the cosy Scottish emotional feel of home,
husband, children and security. Not looked at with any favour by the
suffragettes perhaps, but obviously so bang on target for thousands of
women that the magazine was swiftly followed (as often in the history of
women's magazines) by the launch of a close rival, *Woman's Weekly*, the
first issue of which is recorded as selling half a million copies. Again, it
has survived the decades – eighty years and two world wars and *Woman's
Weekly* is still amongst those present. At one time in the 1970s, *Woman's
Weekly* enjoyed the highest circulation of all women's magazines in this
country. Its editorial formula was always in line with *My Weekly*: the
problem page, the household hints, the knitting patterns, the cookery features. All classic and conventional stuff, perhaps, but the right mixture for
gaining and holding the necessary mass circulation. *My Weekly* is the

second oldest women's magazine still being published in Britain and *Woman's Weekly* the third. The prize for longevity, of course, goes to *The Lady*.

Both these two pre-war weeklies were content with their roles as the housewife's friend. They were more concerned with the sultana roll than suffrage, and child care always came high on their list of priorities. Emancipation was not their interest. This was much more the stock-in-trade of *Woman's Citizen*, which had arrived in 1908 but never made the outbreak of war. Here was the encouragement for women to take the independent view, a title that allowed educated women to interest themselves in politics, industry and intellectual pursuits. But such hard-line polemics found little favour outside a small coterie of bluestockings and committed suffragettes.

As the Great War approached there were probably about fifty women's magazines active on the market. The war was to take its toll on many of the survivors but there was, nevertheless, a firm bedrock of titles in 1914. Not only had women proved to be avid readers of magazines both for information and for entertainment, but the market had discovered the key to success through the decades – to compartmentalize and specialize. The vast and disparate market of women's magazines has always been sustained by its natural divisions: society, domestic, teenage, romantic, fashion, beauty and health. There has always been at least one magazine on the market at any given time to which a woman could relate and with which she might identify. And the broad categories, such as fashion, cookery, and society, have subdivided by readership: demographically, geographically, socially or by age and interest.

In 1911 the American publishing tycoon William Randolph Hearst acquired the existing National Magazine Company in London. The company was purchased from Evelyn Nash, whose sole publication was *Nash's Magazine*, a fiction title in competition with *The Strand*. Hearst's first British venture was a Sunday newspaper, *The London Budget*, based on the American style of separate magazine and comic sections. The paper was unsuccessful but *Nash's* continued through the war, until the 1930s. National Magazines also acquired *Pall Mall* and *Vanity Fair*, but paper rationing thwarted their development. *Vanity Fair* was subsequently used by National Magazines in 1949 as the first young fashion magazine.

Only three of the titles that were being published in Britain at the outbreak of the First World War are still with us today. The war had monumental effects on life and society in this country and the women's magazine business, like so many other industries not directly associated with the war effort, was savagely affected. But the future would bring heartening regeneration and vitality with the attendant triumphs and disasters.

Two

1915–1929

The women's magazine industry was to reflect the radical social changes witnessed in the aftermath of the Great War. As many as 750,000 British men had died in the war and the resultant proliferation of single women had significant editorial effects on some of the magazines. The sweeping economic repercussions of the war dramatically transformed society: some of the rich lost their wealth and many of the lower classes became more affluent, having worked for the war effort in the factories. The girls in domestic service, a diminishing occupation even before the war, were unlikely to be enticed back to work for private families after tasting the freedom and easier life in other forms of work. The middle classes would increasingly have to fend for themselves, with full-time maids often being replaced by 'dailies'.

The war had obviously seen little magazine development but, perhaps ironically, a major title came on to the market in 1916. This was the American magazine *Vogue*, a luxury glossy monthly distinguished by its definitive coverage of high fashion. The British edition arrived during the height of what was probably the darkest time for the British people. The magazine had circulated from America before the war, but as it was hardly a shipping priority, Condé Nast, the American publisher, decided to bring out the British edition.

Today *Vogue* is still the archetypal glossy, the arbiter of *haute couture* and style. It sells over 180,000 copies, considerably outperforming its old American rival *Harper's Bazaar*, known in Britain as *Harpers & Queen*. *Vogue*'s predominance in the market is gradually waning, but its influence in the fashion trade is still indomitable.

The only other new titles recorded during the war were *Girl's Mirror* (1915–33), *Betty's Weekly* (later incorporated into *Woman's Weekly*), *Everywoman's Weekly, Vanity* and *My Paper*. None of these appears to have survived to the Armistice.

The year 1919 saw the launch of *Our Homes & Gardens* from George Newnes. Its modern claim to have been Britain's first home-interest magazine can be disputed by many of the Victorian and Edwardian titles. But it was certainly the first post-war title of any importance, and it set a style for home magazines which has been closely emulated over the years. The editor set the pace in the opening editorial: 'Always we shall strive to avoid the extreme, devoting ourselves instead to what is within the compass of those who think that good taste, expressed in a moderate way, is far more to be desired than what is bizarre and extravagant.'

Homes & Gardens (minus the pronoun) was definitely a quality product, priced at one shilling, and destined for a long life of elegant presentation. Its readers were considered well-off, even if some of them had to live with the 'servant problem' (i.e., no servants). Today, the magazine sells over 150,000 copies, a drop of some twenty-five per cent over the decade, but it still holds a formidable place in the up-market homes category.

The Queen magazine was not too happy about the financial struggle of the old rich, or the new poor. They divided society into four strata: Lady Great House, Lady Newly Rich, Mr and Mrs Badly Off and Mr and Mrs Middle-class. They even showed little surprise that a well-known peeress was negotiating to purchase a modest dwelling in Putney: 'It could scarcely be classed as an aristrocratic quarter, yet during part of the war a marquis lived and died there.' *The Queen* went on:

> People live in such odd places nowadays, in bits of other people's houses, in mews and in parts of their own country houses. The papers are full of advertisements about labour and space-saving furniture as a result of high taxation and high wages, and the dislike of women for domestic work. Food prices and wages of domestic servants are from half to double as much as they were before the war and despite the vast numbers out of work it is almost impossible to obtain servants. The Reds say that domestic service is degrading – what manifest rubbish.

Maybe it was for Mr and Mrs Middle-class, and even perhaps Lady Newly Rich, that Odhams (always a close competitor to Newnes) launched

Ideal Home in 1920. According to its editor, Captain G.C. Clarke, the magazine would cater for 'the wide circle of the middle-class' and 'strive against the erection of hideous houses'. The original title was *The Ideal Home*, but the definite article was soon dropped and replaced by the words 'And Gardening'; this, too, was later deleted. (The magazine had no connection with the *Daily Mail* exhibition of the same name.) In addition to well-designed housing, the magazine covered the usual tips on home management, decoration and furnishing. *Ideal Home* is still on the market today and until the advent of *House Beautiful* in 1989, it was the biggest selling homes magazine in Britain.

The National Magazine Company, not yet a particularly successful Hearst property, now decided that the time was ripe to launch a British version of *Good Housekeeping*. The title had been launched in the United States in 1885 in Springfield, Massachusetts, and was doing well there. William Randolph Hearst bought the magazine in 1911 in a deal that took one hour, with the purchase being made out of future magazine profits. In March 1922, the British edition was launched. The advertisement that appeared in the *Daily Mirror* of 23 February was buoyant:

No magazine to compare with *Good Housekeeping* has ever been attempted in this country before. *Good Housekeeping* would be worth one shilling merely for the splendid stories and superb pictures it contains. It would be worth one shilling merely for the wonderful advance view it gives you of the Spring fashions. It would be worth one shilling merely for the illuminating articles on great Social Questions of interest to every woman. Get it. Read it. See how it helps you in your home, your shopping, in cooking, furnishing, decoration, in the conservation of health and beauty, in the care of children. You will realize that *Good Housekeeping* is infinitely more than a magazine. It is a *New Institution*, destined to play an important part in the lives of thousands of women.

The first issue of 150,000 copies was a sell-out. The ebullient advertising certainly contributed to this instant success. But that success owed a lot to the magazine itself – an all-round title for the middle classes with the usual fiction, cookery, dress-making and practical home help and also erudite articles by Marie Corelli, Clemence Dane, Lady Astor, Rose Macaulay, Violet Bonham Carter, Arnold Bennett and Virginia Woolf. The first issue carried a one-thousand-word frontispiece under the heading

'The Reason for Good Housekeeping', with the italicized motto 'Neither do men light a candle and put it under a bushel, but on a candlestick; and it giveth light onto all that are in the house'.

Good Housekeeping's immediate financial success was a rare event even for those days, to say nothing of modern times. It was making a profit from its third issue and earned enough money during the first few years for Randolph Hearst to purchase St Donat's Castle in Wales. National Magazines had created a classic which was to flourish and grow in stature. Today the magazine is selling over 500,000 copies, the highest in its seventy-two-year history. A master stroke was the opening of the Good Housekeeping Institute two years after the launch, following the same pattern as the American title. This introduced the famous Good Housekeeping Seal of Approval which was to be used for product testing. Although the seal ran into consumer legislation problems in the early 1960s, the expression 'Good Housekeeping Seal of Approval' is still in the vernacular today.

Good Housekeeping concerned itself from the start with the burning issues of the day, particularly as they affected women. Political articles were to the fore, as were regular features and careers for women. Although a celebration of the family and 'the housekeeper', the magazine eagerly developed the cause of the new independence for women and offered advice on how to enjoy the differing roles of wife and mother and working woman. The magazine recognized the massive changes the war had brought to the middle-class reader. As an early article in 1923 explained, 'great movements of mankind, like a European war, which tend to remake the face of the world, can affect women more than they do men, because they leave men where they are, while they make for women a new world with which they must cope'.

Having given its readers food for thought, as well as food, *Good Housekeeping* created a powerful advertising medium in the 1920s, one that flooded in to take advantage of this affluent, responsible readership. Kitchen appliances (to take the place of the missing servants), the developing gas and electric industries, the ubiquitous hot bedtime drinks, laxatives, fashion, department stores, motor cars, toys, bread, soap, children's clothes, food – hundreds of pages of advertising filled this new magazine which ran bigger and bigger issues, and the magazine's publicity crowed with some justification about creating a 'New Institution'. In 1927, the magazine even opened its own restaurant in Oxford Street, and it remained open and successful until the outbreak of war. The London Shopping

Service was another innovation whereby magazine staff would buy items of clothing displayed in the magazine for those readers who were unable to 'get up to town'.

Publishers were again seeking younger readers. In 1919, *Peg's Paper*, the archetypal working-class, simple-story magazine, was specifically targeted towards the shop girl and the mill girl. Here is the blithe editor at work in her first issue:

> It is going to be your weekly pal, girls. My name is Peg, and my one aim in life is to give you a really cheery paper like nothing you've ever read before. Not so very long ago I was a mill girl too. Because I've been a worker like you, I know what girls like, and I'm going to give you a paper to enjoy. Look on me as a friend and helper. I will try to advise you on any problem.

Peg's chatty, all-girls-together approach, which might seem a trifle simplistic and a touch patronizing, represented the secret of so much reader loyalty of this sort of magazine over the years: personal help and one-to-one contact. *Peg* survived until the early days of the Second World War. The whole genre may seem a little naïve today, when young girls' magazines are full of sophisticated sex advice, but for girls in the 1920s and 1930s, this was the quintessential form of literary escape. They loved the elder-sister style and adored the romantic fiction of crinkly-eyed-doctor-on-holiday-meets-shop-girl. Like the pictures, the magazine was a haven of escape from their mundane lives. You could slip off your shoes, open the toffees and float away on a pink cloud of romance. The formula was to be used many times by many magazines and is still with us today.

The magazine industry was beginning to warm up. The early 1920s saw such titles as *Ladies's Home World*, *The Lady's Paper*, *Ladies' Times*, *My Lady Fayre*, *Home Mirror*, *My Favourite*, *Woman of the Day*, *Woman's Kingdom*, *Home Journal* and *Violet Magazine*. It is of some interest that these ephemeral magazines chose titles that were a throwback to the turn of the century, with a continuing emphasis on the word 'Lady'. None of this particular crop survived for long, although *Home Journal* – after a relaunch – reached the outbreak of war before merging into *Woman's Pictorial*.

It was predictable that the 1920s, the era of jazz, the cloche hat, the flapper and the Bright Young Things, would produce its own 'parish' magazine for the gay young girls. In 1920, *Eve* aimed at these daughters of the new rich – overtly and frankly hedonistic. Forget the war, forget the labour unrest, forget the Irish Troubles, ignore the launch of the British Communist Party; this was the time for fun and parties. Skirts were getting shorter, revealing the calves of the legs. The fashion decree in the United States was 'minimum clothes and maximum cosmetics' and in Britain the young flapper strived for the modern look: flat chest, straight clothes and short hair. Corsets were definitely 'out'. So *Eve* was the flappers' house journal – exaggerated pictures and extravagant words. The magazine symbolized the 'roaring twenties', a young girl's breath of fresh air as she dashed from party to party in her sports car and attended all the right social functions. Pleasure was the name of the game: out with all the stuffy old ways and stuffy old people. The magazine almost saw the twenties out but in 1929, perhaps when life got more sombre after the financial crash, it became *Britannia and Eve*, a more sober, standard fashion and beauty title which finally gave up the ghost in 1957.

By now, the title 'Lady' began to give way to the more egalitarian 'Woman'. The label 'Home' continued to be a useful masthead attraction to potential readers. Alfred Harmsworth's Amalgamated Press, prospering with *Woman's Weekly*, saw the opportunity of exploiting the middle-class monthly market by launching *Woman & Home* in 1926. More popular and less cerebral than *Good Housekeeping*, Harmsworth's new magazine was another domestic service title dressed up with the departments that have always decorated women's monthly magazines – knitting, sewing, cookery, gardening. The magazine survives today and up to the launch of the German *Prima* in 1986, it was the top-selling monthly women's magazine. In 1927 *Woman's Journal* entered the market; it inserted the word 'Home' in the middle of its title, only to drop it again when it moved into the world of fashion and beauty. It was always considered up-market and has experienced varied fortunes in its long life. Today its circulation hovers around the 150,000 level and it fits comfortably into the IPC stable as a class act.

Two other titles which were to enjoy long careers were launched in the mid-twenties. *Everywoman* came from Odhams in 1924 and *Modern Woman* from Newnes in 1925, both monthly feature magazines for the middle-class woman. They eventually fell victim to the publishing economics of the 1960s and both were merged into *Woman & Home*, which also incorporates *Modern Home* (1951), *My Home & Family* (1971), and *Good Life* (1980). Mergers are the industry's euphemism for death – a healthier title might incorporate an unsuccessful one. In the rather forlorn hope that readers of the defunct magazine will transfer their allegiance and loyalty to the other title. But they seldom do so, or at least not in any significant numbers. To prevent rival publishers picking up the defunct title, its name must be kept alive on the cover or the contents page of the mother title to imply that it is still in use.

Other new launches in the 1920s were *Wife & Home* in 1929 and *My Home* in 1928. The latter became *My Home & Family* but, as recorded above, it ended its days as part of *Woman & Home*.

In 1922 the market was revived with an American import, *True Story*. The confession genre – down-market, brash and sensational, had long been popular in the States. *True Story* was an instant success in Britain, and was later followed by *True Romances*. There was even romance in the real life story behind the launch of the magazines in this country. An American health fanatic, Bernarr MacFadden, ran Britain's 'Perfect Woman' competition. Mary Williamson, an eighteen-year-old Yorkshire girl, entered the competition, not only winning, but becoming Mrs MacFadden. MacFadden published an American magazine called *Physical Culture*, and Williamson was intrigued by the widespread correspondence its title generated. Many of the letters concerned readers' personal lives and problems and included revelatory details. Mary MacFadden envisaged a magazine with all the stories written in the first person – real-life problems by real-life people: *True Story*. Its immense success in both the United States and Britain soon encouraged the publishers to bring out their own 'me-too', *True Romances*. The editorial ethos of both magazines was true love and idyllic romance, consummated by happy marriage. It is sad to relate (well, it is a true story) that the MacFaddens failed to find married bliss and Mary returned to England, leaving MacFadden to pursue his eccentric life-style. He later parachuted at the age of eighty into the Seine, amongst many other physical exloits.

It is some testimony to the popularity of the genre that *True Romances* and *True Story* are both alive today. They were acquired in 1943 by Argus Press, who still publish them from an address in romantic downtown Streatham. Their circulations are not too dramatic but the demand for romantic editorial seems to continue.

On a rather different plane is the affiliated magazine, exemplified by *Home & Country*, which appeared in 1919 as a little journal of eight pages, with a circulation of 2,000. It is the official magazine of the National Federation of Women's Institutes, with relentlessly domestic editorial and a strong agricultural interest. Today it enjoys a subscription of over 100,000 copies to WI members and has been fortunate to maintain an influential and prestigious link with the Royal family, a connection forged by Queen Mary. Obviously, affiliated magazines are restricted in their outlook, following the party line, but they enjoy the strong advantage of belonging to a membership which created its own solid and steady circulation, away from the squalid commercial publishing world. Hence the long life of *Home & Family*, run since 1888 by the Mothers' Union.

The 1920s was the decade of great expansion as well as constant conflict. The continuing labour problems, capped by the General Strike of 1926, were balanced by the developments in communications.

Good Housekeeping was posing the questions which were easier to ask than to answer. In 1924 Mrs Alfred Sidgwick asked, 'Should Married Women Work?' The editor's note read:

> Thousands of women, everywhere, married women, engaged women, unengaged women, are trying to answer this question. It entails for many of them a choice to be made now, or for the future, between economic freedom and domestic slavery. It is a difficult question, and but rarely has it been discussed so impartially, yet so wisely and helpfully, as by Mrs Alfred Sidgwick. Her article is one no woman should fail to read.

Violet Bonham-Carter, always a powerful campaigner, asked, 'Should Wives Have Wages?' The editor added the caption: 'Even in a coal mine there are shifts. But it is literally true that the work of the working-class wife and mother has no beginning and no end.' Her quoted day was timetabled from '4.30 a.m. Wake husband, who has to be at work by 5 o'clock' through an exhausting day which ended at 8.30 p.m. with 'Clear away and wash up. Get everything ready for the morning. Mend husband's clothes as soon as he gets them off.'

Other vital topics of the day as covered by the magazines: Do Men Want Women in Politics? Have Women a Sense of Humour? Do Women Dress to Please Men? And the thorny question: Should There Be Clubs for Women? (The answer came in later years from Max Kauffmann: 'Only if every other form of persuasion fails!')

Meanwhile, *The Queen* was seeing out the 1920s with a kind of grumpy sniping at the decade's technical achievements. The magazine was very sniffy about the talkies:

It seems that the golden silence of the films is definitely to be broken. Miss Mary Pickford is to make a talking film; a number of English actors are training for the talkies; already the Phonofilm Company here has produced a group of sketches – George Robey for example as a barrister, Ernie Lotinga as a recruit – wherein the slickness of the tongue, combined with action suitable to legal and military life, is intended to deceive the ear. I believe the Phonofilm Company does not intend as yet to produce a long, dramatic picture. The public it is suggested is not ready for it. The question is also whether the talkie is ready for the public and whether given the best of all possible conditions it can ever be an improvement on the silent film.

And the wireless came in for equally superior comment:

Broadcasting is going to save us a lot of trouble, perhaps even that of going to the House of Commons if elected, for in time debates may be carried on through the air. So what if we become slugs? We presume that transmitters providing concerts and so on will send out what 'everybody' wants, or what they think 'everybody' wants, or what they think it would be good for 'everybody' to want, in which case the programmes will consist, not of what is choice and rare, but of what is popular, banal and cheap. Would it pay any business syndicate controlling the wireless lanes of the air to cater for the few, the highly cultured, the discriminating?

The magazine was not fond of the modern school of painting:

Few of the moderns have arrived at a satisfactory solution to their problems. In the pursuit of truth, the abstract is a poor substitute for the concrete. Some go beyond the limits of our intelligibility, some wilfully seek ugliness.

Modigliani found no favour: 'These narrow necks, these prim and tightened mouths, these blank eyes emit an atmosphere of poverty of invention, stupidity and boredom, from which I fly.' And the drama critic was unimpressed with the new play by George Bernard Shaw, starring Sybil Thorndyke:

It may be because I saw *St. Joan* on the second night that the
delicious enthusiasm which has inflamed many other critics of Mr.
Shaw's play and Miss Thorndyke's performance did not touch me at
all. There was not a single moment throughout the whole evening
when the excitement of what was going on on the stage stilled all of
the many coughs which exploded intermittently.

As for literature, *The Queen* loved Aldous Huxley, dismissed Warwick
Deeping and applauded Evelyn Waugh. But, surprisingly, they really preferred the young Beverly Nichols.

And the magazine's epithet for the Jazz Age: 'It is no use fulminating
against jazz. If people want jazz they will have it, and I believe if we let it
run its course (like any other disease) it will perish of its own inanity.'

Woman's Friend, to be more fully peered at later, appeared in 1924
– a nice, chatty, mumsy magazine published by Pearson's at twopence
a week. It had the standard fare of the twopenny weeklies: fiction,
sewing and knitting, little poems, cookery, health, a horoscope and
the ubiquitous problems page. It was modest, successful and ran until
1950 when it merged with *Glamour*. *Woman's Companion*,
another weekly, was launched in 1927 by Amalgamated Press. It survived the years, finally succumbing in 1961 when it merged with
Woman's Weekly. D.C. Thomson, up there in Dundee, were still keeping their place in the women's magazine race (*People's Friend, My
Weekly*) and in 1929 produced *Red Star*, a weekly for the younger
market and a companion to *Red Letter*, which they had published
since the turn of the century.

The last major launch of the decade was another American import,
Harper's Bazaar. This fashion glossy dated back to 1867 in the USA but
had slipped back severely in the market-place there with the advent and
exploitation of *Vogue*. William Randolph Hearst purchased the title from
the House of Harper in 1911 for $10,000. His editorial panacea for the
ailing magazine was to put the art editor in charge, making the text
secondary to the illustrations. The prestige and circulation of *Harper's
Bazaar* rose steadily with its emphasis on European fashion until it had
become a worthy and marketing competition to *Vogue*. The two had
battled out the market through the 1920s and it was perhaps inevitable
that the National Magazine Company should throw their (elegant, of
course) hat into the ring in this country to challenge the superiority that
Vogue had built up since its introduction thirteen years before.

Harper's Bazaar, from its 1929 launch right through the next decade, was a supremely elegant production, from the exquisite front covers by Erté, through its coverage of the fashions of international designers like Patou, Lanvin, Chanel, Molyneux, Revillon and Worth, to its overtly snobbish interest in society – definitely with a capital 'S'. The magazine was printed on paper of superb quality, attracted high-class advertising and bore a cover price of two shillings, double that of the quality home magazines like *Homes & Gardens* and *Ideal Home*. The name *Vanity Fair* was carried on the mast head, a franchise jealously guarded by the Hearst Corporation since the original political satire title with its Spry cartoons had died in 1912. *Harper's* was particularly strong on fiction by the top authors of the day with Evelyn Waugh, Lord Dunsany, Ben Travers, Osbert Sitwell, Wyndham Lewis and Somerset Maugham being typical contributors. All the fashion pictures were drawn with elegant artistry – no fashion photography.

The society pages were manifestly establishment. The main social feature, a predecessor of 'Jennifer's Diary', was 'The Mirror of London' by Atalanta. The pages were liberally sprinkled with aristocratic names and every move of the Royals was faithfully recorded.

A good many changes have taken place in London while holidaymakers have been away. There has sprung up in London a little group of new theatres, one of the prettiest of which is the Cambridge in Seven Dials and there have been additions to our public buildings and a number of new amusements in the shape of miniature golf courses.... Americans have stayed longer in London than usual and are only now returning home. For them the chefs at our big hotels have been devising new dishes. One which met with considerable approval is oysters cooked in brandy – a dish which would bring a shudder to the real gourmet. The tendency to cook oysters is unfortunately growing among foreign chefs.... All the royalties will be down from Deeside, as their busy times begin this month. The Prince of Wales, who caught a bad cold flying in Scotland in a mist before he went to Le Touquet, has a heavy list of engagements.... The Duke of York has many engagements for the future and meantime his house is being put in order for the homecoming of the Duchess and the blue-eyed Princess Margaret Rose who is to have a new nursery. The Duchess is having a pleasant time buying new clothes, which she has had to deny herself for some time.

The magazine was always alert to the Latest Thing:

> WONDER BAR, with its pretty green setting and glass topped tables
> that light up when patrons are seated, has been a big attraction since
> its first night, which was notable for its surprises on the stage as
> well as in the audience, where the first divided evening skirt made its
> appearance on a charming patron.... The United Hunt Ball at the
> Savoy on the fifteenth promises to be a great affair, with two
> thousand guests gathered from every hunt in the country, the supper
> tables decorated with the colours of the various hunts and the band
> dressed for the occasion in hunting pink.

The leading columns could also take on a toffee-nosed sniff, like this
realization that blocks of flats had to be shared with other people – unlike
one's country place:

> There is a great unrest in our midst over the question of a home. Far
> too many of us are homeless. We live in glorified tenements, chock-
> a-block with Tom, Dick and Harry and their wives and their friends.
> We hear their radios, their laughter, and the sounds they make when
> they have 'company' though we may ignore them when we meet in
> the lift. Their servants are our servants; their lift is our lift; their page
> boy and porter are ours too. But worst of all their noise is our noise.

Harper's Bazaar was the final notable launch of the decade. There is
an irony that the world's leading two fashion glossies, aimed at the super
rich, should both have been launched in this country at times of the
greatest international crisis. *Vogue* was brought out in 1916 at the worst
period of the Great War, and *Harper's* saw the light of day in the year of
the Wall Street Crash and the beginning of the devastating Depression on
both sides of the Atlantic. With its unusually long pages (about thirteen
inches), it was a welcome addition to the reading matter of the upper-class
woman. It knew what it was about and it made no compromise.

Harper's was hardly typical of the magazine business, nor of the interests and social conditions of ninety-nine per cent of the population. It
may have been fun-time at the Savoy but the rest of Britain, and the
magazine industry, was to face a decade of continuing depression, mass
unemployment, pockets of grinding poverty, international unrest on a grand
scale and threatening war clouds.

Three

1932–1938

Having won so many victories for their status, particularly in the work place, it was ironic for women that unemployment was one of the national ills of the 1930s. The TUC, having approved the proposed concept of child benefits, also objected to 'the invasion of industry by women'. Women civil servants voted in favour of women's compulsory retirement on marriage.

The employed family man on £1000 a year could live well with his family. New homes were being advertised in the women's magazines for as little as £700 freehold. Ford produced the £100 car and new products, like the refrigerator, were pouring on to the market at affordable prices.

Good Housekeeping concerned itself with the family budget in article after article. It loved quoting sample budgets, possibly as a paradigm for its seemingly profligate readers. In December 1931, out of a selection of the middle-class with earned incomes from £500 to £1500 a year, the magazine ran a competition (first prize – a £10 cheque) to hear about the economies readers were effecting. The 'Business Man on £1000' was a sample budget:

Business Man (two adults, two grown-up daughters – one at college, one maid kept).

Earned income of	£1000
Income Tax	£106
Rates & Property Tax	£120
Household Expenses	
(To include food, wages laundry, light & fuel)	£326

Education	£100
Clothing, personal allowance, charity	£170
Holidays, amusement and car	£130
Insurance	£25
Incidental expenses, doctor, dentist, etc.	£23
	£1000

Higher up the social scale, *The Queen* was glum. 'The pessimists call us to prepare for the worst; that the world depression has by no means reached its climax and that we have many anxious months, possibly years, ahead.' But a look through the pages of the magazine shows no particular signs of poverty or depression. The Season went on with its customary glitter and excitement. The magazine reported all the latest rages and crazes like face-lifting, electric stimulants, diets, the new cosmetics and the fad for psychology. They were enthusiastic about the new King and Queen in 1937 and decidedly sniffy about the abdication; they managed to ignore the existence of Mrs Simpson.

With the notable exceptions of *Woman's Own* (1932) and *Woman* (1937), there was surprisingly little new magazine activity in the decade. There was a flurry of romantic fiction titles: *Secrets* (1932), *Oracle* (1933) *Lucky Star* and *Miracle* (1935) and *Glamour* in 1938. These half-grown-up comics had an ingenuous and moral tone but they must have helped to make mundane life more bearable for a generation of poorly paid girls with routine jobs and prosaic boy friends. To the fictional dream world would be added the expected formula of horoscopes and fortune telling. For twopence you could buy a lot of dreams.

You could also live out your fantasies in the cinema, then at the height of its popularity. The market obliged with plenty of film magazines, mostly of a fanzine nature, and these must have been read by our would-be romantics. In 1935 came a title expressly aimed at the fair sex, *Woman's Filmfair*, which looked at films from a woman's viewpoint. It was to run for a few years until the war took its toll.

Woman's Own came from Newnes in 1932, billed as 'the new big-value weekly for the up-to-date wife and wife-to-be'. It was accompanied by free gifts and a supplement printed by the new photo-tone process. The target audience was lower middle-class women living in small homes, and the new magazine carried articles on domesticity, cookery, beauty advice, baby care, knitting, true-to-life fiction and help with personal problems. Not an entirely new formula but notable for the confidence of its launch from Newnes and its undoubted success which would soon lead to me-too publications from the two mass magazine rivals Odhams and Amalgamated Press. *Woman's Own* set a style and a speed which dominated the women's magazine market for over fifty years, with massive profits and unheard-of circulation figures.

The issue of 21 July 1934 was typical of the period. It consisted of thirty-six pages for twopence. The editor opened the magazine with an anecdotal page. Sample snippet:

A HELPFUL WORLD

There is something rather nice about the helpfulness of strangers these days. I had yet another sample of it this week – this time on a London 'bus.

I got on and proceeded to get my penny ready – only to find I hadn't one. No manner of searching would produce anything smaller then a ten-shilling note.

Very embarrassing! However, I explained the situation to the conductor, apologising and asking him whether, by chance, he could change the note. Check-mate – he couldn't, having just come on duty. While I was offering him a stamp as the only means of payment left, a fellow traveller opened her bag and tendered me the necessary penny! At the same moment the conductor – honest man – offered me a halfpenny change out of my three-halfpenny stamp – wasn't that nice of both of them?

Rather remarkable to an old cynical publisher like me that such an august lady editor should have travelled by bus!

Nine of the editorial pages were devoted to fiction. 'Oh, Honeybee! It was the dickens of a mess – Jane and Trevor had only been married a few hours when he lost his job!' Play Girl: 'Can Rosalind go through with her promise to Bob? The fact that it was for Roddy's sake gave her strength!' Father's Race: 'It was really too bad of Bill to be late home today! For small Humphrey had specially asked him to the sports.'

The rest is cookery, letters with an etiquette bias, patterns, plans for a caravan holiday, novelty knits and a spread on British films and Uncle John's page for the Woman's Own Cheeribles. Eight pages were advertising.

The distinguishing mark between *Woman's Own* and its earlier competitors was the inclusion of an eight-page section 'incorporated by means of Bell Punch Company's Intersetter'. The section had a heavy sepia appearance but stood out from the remaining letter-press pages like a sore thumb. Photogravure was a few years away, but it was the new printing processes which finally helped to sound the death knell for so many of the titles left over from the 1920s. *Woman's Own* went on to have an impressive history as one of Britain's top-selling magazines – in the 1950s it reached a zenith circulation of nearly three million.

Woman's Illustrated was the first reply by Amalgamated Press to the success of *Woman's Own*. It launched in 1936 with the same formula, but it never caught the success of either *Woman's Own* or the imminent *Woman*. At the outbreak of war the circulation was only 150,000, but it showed a steady climb in the post-war years, peaking at 900,000 in 1958. But even this figure compared poorly to *Woman* and *Woman's Own*, then at their highest circulation levels. *Woman's Illustrated* died in 1961, when Odhams merged it with *Woman*.

Odhams' first challenge to the other new weeklies was to launch *Mother* in 1936, a magazine with an obvious specific target audience. Perhaps Odhams rather over-iced the cake when they announced that *Mother* would be 'the greatest occasion of the century in magazine journalism for women'. No magazine could expect to live up to that sort of hype, even without the limitations of the title. By the outbreak of war it was selling a lowly 115,000 copies, and although Odhams made considerable efforts during the baby boom years to vivify it the magazine was sold in 1990 to the burgeoning EMAP, who then strategically closed it.

The significance of the 1937 launch of *Woman* cannot be overemphasized. Odhams owned the new photogravure printing plant at Watford, a factory prepared for the printing of their big national weekly title, *John Bull*. It was inevitable that Odhams should produce a big women's weekly to compete with the other two entrants, and it must also have seemed obvious that with their new modern process the title would be printed gravure. Overnight they would make the existing weeklies look drab and colourless and comparatively poor value for money. By going gravure they were immediately in the big numbers game. The gravure process, using sixty-four-page cylinders, not only produces superior quality printing but does it at lightning speed. The 'make-ready', or machine set-up process is expensive, but once the rotary machines are started, copies can be run off at great speed by the million. The more copies run, the cheaper the unit cost. For the first time, a woman's magazine appeared in the same mass market as the newspapers, but with an infinitely superior product. The great bonus that transformed the women's magazines was colour, and that meant mass advertising. Magazines moved towards the opulent domain of the big national colour advertisers, and away from the petty letterpress world of the 1920s magazines, with their low print-runs and correspondingly low appeal to national advertisers.

Woman, a truly national magazine, aimed to reach a cross-section of women all over the country. The editor declared that it sought to entertain as well as to give practical help and advice for the home. The magazine also maintained that it had a mission:

> *Woman* is here to help you in every way possible. Consult her in all your troubles and perplexities, no matter what they may be. We provide for you reliable advice on almost every question under the sun. At the head of the list stand several subjects of particular interest to women. Here we place Woman's Council of Seven at your service.

For all its promised splendours, the magazine was a slow starter and failed to reach the guarantee it had given to its advertisers. But by the outbreak of war it had climbed to a satisfactory 750,000 copies, and in time it was to make history as the highest-selling women's weekly ever.

The magazine was notable for its advice columns, edited by Evelyn Home, the *nom de plume* of Peggy Makins. She ran the letters page for decades, her eventual successor being Virginia Ironside. In the fiftieth anniversary issue of the magazine, published in 1987, the style and content of half a century of readers' problems were compared. Evelyn Home quoted one of her early letters:

A DIFFICULT PROBLEM

Dear Evelyn Home,

I've been trying to pluck up courage to write to you for a long time now, and at last I have. I do hope you will be able to help me.

I have been going out with a young man for over a year (I am eighteen, he is four years older) and we are deeply in love with each other. The trouble is that he is very passionate and I am not at all demonstrative, and he once told me he was afraid I would be just as cold when we were married.

Once he implored me so desperately to yield to him just once that I gave in, but I was terribly disappointed. I experienced none of the joy or thrill that is supposed to come with intercourse, and I don't believe my boy did either. It may have been because I was not specially willing, but I am afraid I shall be just the same when we are married.

We have both been very sad about this and my boy gets awfully nervy and miserable about it. I wish I could help him, but somehow I can't. Do advise me.

Evelyn never hung back with advice:

I am so glad you wrote to me, my dear. Although it was a great mistake of yours to give way to your boyfriend, it has taught you one thing – that the privileges of matrimony can very rarely be truly enjoyed by those who have not been properly married.... Your boy has no need to work himself up into such a state of uncontrolled nerves. He should find strength in the thought that you are preserving an infinitely precious thing that will forever brighten your life together after you are married.... Meanwhile, give yourselves fewer opportunities for lovemaking, go about with a crowd and enjoy yourselves in more innocent pastimes until you appreciate the full significance of love and marriage.

Evelyn followed the party line for thirty-eight years. Her pseudonym had been carefully chosen by a qualified psychologist originally employed to run the problem page. 'Eve' was intended to hint at the temptress, while the 'Home' was the ambition of every woman. Virginia Ironside (whose real name could have been invented by the same psychologist) had to experience much more modern problems, including AIDS, contraception, racial complications and all the social diseases. Her advice was always sound:

OPEN MARRIAGE

I've often suggested to my husband we have an open marriage. Not because I really want one but because I like to hear him saying it would be out of the question it makes me feel secure. But the last time I suggested it, hoping for the usual reassurance, he said: 'Fine,' and now I find he's slept with his secretary three times. I have been so unhappy I don't know what to do. He said it meant nothing and it wouldn't have occurred to him to do anything if I hadn't seemed so keen on the idea. He wishes he could put the clock back, says it was purely physical, and that she was a dreadful girl and he only strung her along. This has made me feel worse because he must be so callous to behave like that to her.

Virginia cracked in:

Good heavens – you can't have it both ways! He's done as you asked and you can't blame him for taking you seriously. Now he's trying to repair the damage by saying it meant nothing to him and you blame him for being callous! It sounds to me as if you are terribly insecure and unhappy and perhaps both of you should seek marriage counselling to sort out your feelings about each other.

In the meantime, back in the thirties, the other weeklies were struggling on in their more modest letterpress livery. *Woman's Friend*, which had been launched by Pearson's in 1924 and saw the war out, was still a flourishing title. It's a diversion to look at a copy of the magazine published on 1 January 1938. It still cost twopence but looked pale and wan beside copies of the more robust *Woman* and *Woman's Own* of that year. There was plenty of fiction ('The woman who stays at home... does she wonder about the women who don't? About the women her husband meets during office hours? A story that will appeal to every wife'), a Nova Pilbeam interview, a jumper knitting pattern, a serial by Lady Troubridge, some party dishes (Macaroni and turkey *réchauffé*), 'Your Fate for 1938' from the cards, 'Jane's Journal', a day in the life of an ordinary housewife, and 'Ask Susan March' (red face, wart inside nose and constipation were three of the problems). The editor was enthusiastic in her own page, Let us Gossip, about the Royal Family. She could not resist a bit of royal chit-chat:

TWEEDS FOR THE PRINCESSES

A reminder that the Princess Elizabeth and Margaret Rose are growing up into big girls will, I've just been told, be given by new winter coats that are being made for them to wear after Christmas.

These coats are more substantial than the little Princesses have worn up to now. They're being made of real honest-to-goodness Harris Tweed, from some length of the fragrant homespun which the Queen bought for herself at a recent exhibition. One pattern that particularly pleased Her Majesty was a black and white dog-tooth check – rather like the Scots 'Shepherds Plaid'. It's likely I hear that some of this length will be made up for the Princesses.

Madame Wanda, the 'famous Hollywood fortune teller', and Nell St John Montague, 'the society clairvoyant', were given a whole spread to impress or depress the reader with the cards. Jane, pictured in pearls and twinset, reports the doings in the life of an ordinary housewife. Her opening paragraph describes the family's Christmas morning – an orgy of parcels. Breakfast was enlivened by the appearance of Mrs Jenkins, the daily:

Cat is sick in hall, and Mrs. Jenkins arrives to tell me she wishes me a merry Christmas mum, and all the best I could wish myself. Present her with handsome tip and she smiles and says thank you, it's a God send and she doesn't care 'oo knows it. Feel moved to give her various small oddments in my larder, and also pair of dark grey knickers, just received from Aunt Agatha who says, I never wear enough and she hopes I like them. Feel impelled to shake Mrs. Jenkins by the hand, and she says warmly she knows a lady when she sees one, and there are some she could mention swankers down this very road who never 'ave their 'ands out of dish water if the truth was to be known. Smile and pat hair, hoping that I look ready for Court circles, and show her out.

Dr Mary was the advice lady. In 1938, Mrs A. of Rotherham had a communication problem:

My daughter is rather a reserved girl and has a nice young man. They want to get married but she is very innocent and asks me how babies come and things she should know. Being shy myself I can't explain, and reading your talks I hope you can help me to get some kind of an illustrated book which will help her to know these things.

And Joan Summers was the leader of a band of housewives who met every week on page 29. Her first questioner, Mary Brown, consulted her with a real problem: 'How can I be certain of keeping my party frock clean when washing up on Christmas Day?' The answer was obvious: 'By wearing an old mackintosh coat instead of your overall. Button the coat right up to the neck and you are absolutely safe.'

The best advice of all was reserved for the last page, where wisdom was dispensed by The Shadow Woman, pictured by the glow of a fireside. 'Don't you feel it easier to discuss your problems in the flickering light of a fire?' Marian sought her advice on a ticklish problem. 'I was introduced to a young man the other night and want to go on with the acquaintance. Can you tell me who speaks first?' The Shadow Woman whipped back: 'I suppose you mean who recognizes the other or speaks first on meeting again. That is your privilege. If you wish to go on with the acquaintanceship smile and speak when you next meet. That shows him you desire to be friends.'

Woman's Pictorial, which had been going since 1919, was another Amalgamated Press production, with the same ingredients as *Woman's Friend*. There was a royal flavour as well as romantic stories and a strong maternal element. Leonora Eyles was the Agony Aunt. But by the mid-thirties the style and format were beginning to look very familiar and the letterpress production looked jaded. It is easy to see why Odham's felt so confident about moving into photogravure.

Some evidence of the inter-war years style in editorial can be gleaned by looking at the Agony Aunt letters. No weekly magazine eschewed the device of the problem page, which made very readable copy and, incidentally, provided free editorial. It has always been part of the credo of popular women's magazines that they enjoy a special relationship with their readers – the editor and the reader on a one-to-one basis. Even young Mr Beeton, the progenitor of *The Queen*, was not above running Cupid's Letter Bag in *Englishwoman's Domestic Magazine* back in 1852. Short shrift, however, was given to Jessie of Brompton when she queried:

I am about to be married but am sorely afraid of being compelled to give up going to balls and routs, of which I am excessively fond. My intended husband is of a very quiet turn of mind while I have a great taste for pleasure... under these circumstances could I be happy?

The reply was frosty: 'We are quite sure that if Jessie could be happy her husband would not... let Jessie remain single until she can learn regard of self.'

Home Chat in the 1920s was shocked by a reader's innocence: 'I am sorry I cannot answer so intimate a question through these columns, and I am rather amazed at your ignorance about the facts of life. Ask an older friend to tell you.'

But by the 1930s, the accent was on tender care and regard for the reader. It was a very competitive time for the Agony Aunts! Nevertheless, there was a touch of astringency in the reply to Doris in *Home Journal* in 1934:

> I am twenty-eight and have had five men friends since I was twenty. I have thrown them all over because they insisted on kissing me. I want to get married and have a home but I can't stand a man touching me. Is there anything wrong with me?

The comforting reply came from Mary Forrest:

> Yes, a great deal; your mind must have been poisoned against men and nature generally. You certainly ought not to marry feeling the way you do; you would make some man's life a misery and not be happy yourself. If you write to me privately I will explain things to you, and then perhaps you may feel differently about everything.

Home Journal, 1934, again:

> I am getting married shortly and only learnt from a girl friend last night that this may mean I shall have a baby. I am horrified about it all. Surely things can't be so horrible as she says? Will you say something to comfort me?

The reply was urgent: 'Please will you send me your address at once. The truth is not horrible at all; your friend has been trying to frighten you.'

The sadly mistaken *Woman's Own* in 1934: 'I am engaged to the nicest boy in the world but am suffering from my terror of war; I get into positive panics in case there will be a war and he will be killed.' The reply was conciliatory:

I think most of us who think at all feel like this. I know I do when I think of my son and my girls' young men. We can only hope that, if people think progressively the next great war will be prevented by arbitration. Join the League of Nations Union, then you will feel that you are doing something to prevent war. It's no use sitting down to worry; do something definite, then you will feel better.

Woman's Pictorial in 1935 received a worried plea:

I am going to be married shortly to a man who was engaged for some time to another woman. She broke the engagement long before I met him, but now has turned up again and says that, as she has his ring, she can still make him marry her. He is terribly frightened she will sue him for breach of promise as he had no proof that it was she who broke the engagement, and we are both worried to death.

The reply was soothing:

Really, I don't think you have anything to worry about. If the woman had not seen your fiancé for some considerable time before you met him, it is most unlikely that she would be successful if she brought a breach of promise case now. If, however, you still feel anxious, why not consult a solicitor? This will cost very little and your minds will be set at rest.

The correspondent to *Lady's Companion* in 1937 was bitter:

I feel that the marriage laws are all wrong. My husband has been calling on another woman, though I have worked hard all my life, helped to make the home, and have saved money. Now I have a broken heart. I tell my husband the best thing he can do is to go and drown himself. I wish he would.

Lady's Companion showed little sympathy:

I realise that when you wrote to me you were beside yourself, but still, however badly you may feel, there is no virtue in wishing anybody dead. If you are as violent as this, then it is quite obvious why your husband became interested in somebody else. Can't you realise that there may be nothing in it at all, and that you are exaggerating the whole case? My dear, your life lies at the parting of the ways, and I implore you not to fly at it like this. I beg you to think and to sit down quietly and review the situation. Realise that men do have passing fancies, and I am afraid you must understand this. Men and women are not alike on some points, and even if you do disagree with what I say, I must be sincere and truthful. Never for one moment do I condone the erring husband, because I know too well the pain and heartbreak that he gives, but I do urge you to make the best and not the worst of your life.

A lady with a problem to *Woman's Own* in 1934: 'Can you advise me about a hat? It is a nightmare to me to buy hats as I have long hair and can never get one to fit; I also wear glasses, and that makes me look repulsive in a hat. What can I do?' The reply gave her short shrift:

A good many people wear glasses, but they don't make them look repulsive. It is often difficult for a young person with long hair to buy a hat. The only thing is to have them made if you can find a milliner to make them for you; or to cut your hair, which I would think would be the wisest thing.

A plea from Walham Green to *Woman's Friend* in 1938:

I have been happily married for two years, but the other day discovered that for three months my husband has been very friendly with a girl at the shop where he buys his cigarettes. A friend told me she had seen them walking across the park near our house, and I have noticed several things which make me feel dreadfully jealous. I know this girl, she is rather pretty, and we used to play tennis at the same club. Can you advise me what to do?

The reply seemed sensible, although the word 'stalk' seems a bit steep:

Don't grow suspicious. Some men like to stalk girls and there may be nothing wrong. But as you know her, and evidently have been quite friendly why not cultivate her acquaintance too? If you are friendly with her and he sees this, the inclination to seek her out may pass.

Suppose you find a young man and make a foursome. You could invite her to your house occasionally. Keep your end up by being particularly charming and nice and never let your husband suspect that you feel jealous.

These letters may seem risibly naïve today but a glance at our contemporary weeklies shows that the subjects and problems have changed little. Sex, boyfriends, relationships, mothers-in-law, marriage problems, infidelity – all the stuff of the Agony Aunts. The difference is in the style. The replies these days are disarmingly frank; the famous Dr Delvin considerably flavoured the pages of *She* magazine in the 1970s and 1980s. Jessie, and Doris, and Mrs T. of Walham Green are still out there crying for help. Writing to women's magazines is so often the solution to their worries, even though the more boring and sensible of us might feel a visit to a doctor or a solicitor or a marriage counsellor might seem more appropriate.

Good Housekeeping and the other shilling home magazines were still struggling along with their middle-class problems. Not for them the Agony Aunts – but they certainly addressed one hundred and one questions about running the home. *Homes & Gardens* ran a page of handy hints from readers; the favourite subject appeared to be removing ink from carpets. The magazine also recommended the installation of a family medicine chest with a suggestion for its contents: 'Permanganate of potash is an invaluable disinfectant and deodoriser. A solution of it can be used for testing the purity of water, as it will turn bad water brown. Mustard for baths and poultices, and mustard leaves for chest ailments.' *Homes & Gardens* readers suffered from their servants, when they had them. There was a complaint about the cook:

Can you tell me the reason of my cook's continuous failure with steamed soufflé puddings? She tells me they are invariably light and 'up' when she is about to dish them, but equally invariably they sink directly she puts them on to the dish, so that they arrive at the table collapsed and in a 'sad' condition.

Homes & Gardens suggested a Pyrex serving dish rather than a sprint from kitchen to dining room.

But thousands of readers of the quality monthlies had no cook, with or without collapsed soufflés. Now that so often the servants were no more, or were reduced to daily visits, there was a great thirst from the respectable homes of the country for information on myriad household topics. *Good Housekeeping* ran a monthly feature called The House-keeper's Dictionary of Facts, which was compiled from readers' enquiries and answered by the Good Housekeeping Institute. Sometimes, though, the questions came from the domestic staff: 'Many thanks for the recipe for Golden Twirls. They were very successful and my mistress was so charmed with your prompt response that she has placed a regular order for your magazine at the village newsagents here.'

Everything from removing tea stains from a blanket, to feeding kitchen waste to fowls, to renovating fire-grates, to mending a teapot handle, to weighing golden syrup – month by month the treasury of household wisdom unfolded.

But the shilling monthlies were still preoccupied by the servant problem. Sometimes the problem meant no servants but sometimes it referred to the age-old question of poor servants, or girls who got impertinent and 'above their station'. Even in February 1930, an article lamenting the good old days when servants knew their place (which was preferably in your house) moaned about the situation:

In many ways, however, the problem has never been so acute as it is at the moment. Without taking too seriously the lamentations of the Victorian dowagers of Mayfair and Kensington, we may still admit that this difficulty is perhaps the most urgent that the modern woman has to face.

I am not thinking of the rich woman. In her case the traditional servile heirarchy of the great house can still be kept up with its elaborate ritual and division of labour. I am thinking rather of the general run of the middle classes, people who, in a family of two children, keep a cook and a nurse and consider themselves, as indeed they are, hopelessly understaffed. I have also in mind a class that is essentially modern and rapidly increasing, a most important class because it is forward-looking and is giving the cue to oncoming generations. This is the small but vigorous group of professional or semi-professional women who are also wives and mothers. Theirs is the hardest case of all; for them the servant problem raises issues that are sometimes all but tragic.

Maids, however, had not completely disappeared in the middle-class home in the middle of the 1930s. It was another four years before much

of the available young labour force, once traditionally in domestic service, departed with speed and gratitude into the munition factories, the
women's services or the Land Army. What a fundamental sea-change
took place in the lives of these young women, who were never to return
to the life 'below stairs'. Their places in the houses of the more affluent
were eventually taken by an army of willing Filipinos after the war. But
if you got hold of some pliable material in 1935, a girl from the country
whom you could work into the ground and trust not break the dishes,
you turned once again to the magazines for help and illumination.

Good Housekeeping ran a short series on Training a General Maid.
'Good servants are made, not born,' said the magazine, 'and need teaching if they are to be efficient.'

Everyone will have her own ideas regarding details of training a
young maid, but this article, based on the actual practical experience
of one of our readers, should prove helpful. As with all successful
teaching, a considerable amount of patience is demanded when
training a maid, and it is here that the fussy, nervous type of
mistress often fails. A reader wrote to the Institute recently
complaining bitterly of her maid, but when one had finished reading
the letter, one could not but sympathise with the girl. Every minute
speck of dust irritated the mistress, in fact, she had stairs and all
main rooms dusted twice daily, once before and once after luncheon.
This is probably an extreme case, but it is an instance of the
unreasonable demands sometimes made. Dissatisfaction and lack of
co-operation in the household are bound to develop in such
circumstances.

The magazine was kind enough to publish its suggestions for the daily
routine of the successful applicant to the position of General Maid.

THE DAY'S ROUTINE.

The maid should rise not later than half-past six or a quarter to
seven, so that she can start work punctually at seven. She should
open up the house, drawing blinds and curtains and opening the
windows.

Her work should then be arranged more or less as follows:

Lay the fire in the dining-room.
Sweep and dust room.

7.15.	Light gas stove, fill kettle and put on stove to boil for early tea.
7.30.	Call master and mistress. Complete dusting of hall.
8.0.	Lay table and cook breakfast.
8.30.	Dining-room and kitchen breakfast.
9.0.	Clear away, wash up; tidy and sweep kitchen. Clean front door-steps etc., if not done before breakfast. Assist mistress make beds, sweep and dust bedroom. Clean bathroom and lavatory.
	Sweep and dust lounge, if this is not undertaken by mistress.
11.0.	Special work.
12.45.	Lay the luncheon table.
1.0.	Lunch.
1.45.	Clear away lunch, wash up; clean and tidy kitchen.
2.30.	Free time until 4.30, to go out or stay in as she pleases, but in any case not on duty.
4.30.	Prepare and take in afternoon tea.
5.0.	Wash up; commence preparations for dinner.
7.0.	Lay table for dinner.
7.30.	Dinner. Wait at table.
8.0.	Bring coffee into sitting-room. Clear away and wash up. Turn down beds and fill hot water bottles if required.

Maybe it was no coincidence, or else a tribute to the advertisement department's sense of humour, that the adjacent advertisement to this editorial was for Yeastamin, the tonic to cure digestive orders, neuritis, rheumatism, constipation, insomnia, sciatica and anaemia!

The women's magazines were beginning to reap the benefits of the advertising industry's media expenditure. As the successful titles grew in circulation and influence, building up targeted readerships and introducing the magic ingredient of colour, so their pages were rewarded with more and more advertising. There was no television, no commercial radio, no colour in newspapers, no Sunday supplements, no cinema advertising. Media competition was confined to monotone newspapers and outdoor hoardings. It was natural, therefore, and commercially sensible for the big food and beauty advertisers to flock to the photogravure mass weeklies like *Woman* and the quality advertisers to the shilling monthlies.

Products for the home were the focus of such quality titles as *Ideal Home*, *Homes & Gardens* and *Good Housekeeping*. A run through their pages in the last half of the 1930s shows a preponderance of motoring advertising. Ford ran a monthly page with copy beamed towards women – and never repeated the same advertisement. Vauxhall were other heavy users of the magazines ('Streaming down the Great West Road – Two Thousand Cars an Hour! Today there are nearly half a million cars on Britain's Roads.') BP ('Banishes Pinking!') and Shell were constant advertisers. Laxatives were a ubiquitous product in all the women's magazines – Bile Beans and Ex-Lax being, if you pardon the expression, very regular. Hot drinks were prevalent; the whole of Britain seemed to go to bed with a steaming mug of Horlicks, Ovaltine, Bovril, Oxo and the rest. Hoover and Electrolux slugged it out model by model. Hoover, in particular, made a virtue out of their latest model as a most welcome Christmas or birthday present for the wife.

Alcohol never seemed to appear in any of the magazines but cigarettes were everywhere. They were always on offer at Christmas-time in splendid seasonal packs. Will's Gold Flake would sell you an oak cabinet of one hundred cigarettes for ten shillings and sixpence or in cedarwood for nine shillings and sixpence. McDougalls sold their self-raising flour in full colour advertisements with recipes on the backing page for the steamed puddings printed on the obverse. The new refrigerators – the middle-class status symbol of the 1930s – were persistent advertisers. You could buy a bungalow at Peacehaven for £400 freehold or rent one of the new luxury flats in London's Dolphin Square for £100 per annum. All the great and famous brand names graced the pages of the women's magazines. Schweppes Cider quenched your thirst, Grape Nuts offered you a healthy morning glow. Viyella kept you warm, Celanese kept you cool, Sunlight Soap kept you clean, Bronco gave you silky comfort, Hornby and Triang tempted your children, Bisto flavoured your food, Icilma kept your skin smooth, Elizabeth Arden and Helena Rubinstein made you beautiful, Benger's recuperated you, Virol looked after growing girls, Robin starched your table-cloth, Gorringes kitted out your schoolchildren, Eno's pepped you up, Pelmanism concentrated your mind, Vita-Wheat kept you slim, Aga cooked your food, Drages furnished your home, Mr Therm heated it and Horlicks prevented night starvation. Singer sewed your clothes, Rendells stopped unwanted children, Permutit softened your water, Sanderson decorated your walls, Lifebuoy kept you smelling nice, Pedigree wheeled your babies, Silvo cleaned the silver, Persil washed your clothes, Shamphams made your sandwiches, Ideal Milk fed your baby, Reckitt's Blue was white, Atora made your puddings and Foster Clark's your custard.

The only other magazine titles to record for the 1930s were a disparate group with mixed fortunes. Most of them barely reached the outbreak of war, let alone survived it. *Ladies' Only* (1933–5), *Miss Modern* (1935–40), *Woman's Fair* (1935–41) and *Woman's Mirror*, which launched in 1934 and was merged the following year with *Woman's World*. The only long-liver was Newnes' *Woman & Beauty*, launched in 1930, presumably as a rival to *Woman's Journal*, from Amalgamated Press. It survived until 1963. At the time of its demise the circulation was down to a paltry 73,000.

The last gasp from the industry before the outbreak of war came from the new publishing house, Hulton Press. Edward Hulton, whose father had owned the *Evening Standard*, launched the photo weekly *Picture Post* in 1938. It was a much superior product to Odhams' *Weekly Illustrated*, which had pioneered the British picture paper earlier in the 1930s. Employing top photographers and journalists, *Picture Post*'s golden days were to come with the war with its famous and sensational coverage of the home front and the war overseas. Hulton had also launched *Lilliput*, the classic magazine for men, and had bought out *Farmer's Weekly*. The Hulton Press's interest in the women's field was generated by the launch of *Housewife* in 1939. It adopted the pocket-size format, like its stablemate *Lilliput*, but later moved up to a more conventional page size, probably at the insistence of the advertisers. *Housewife* set out with style and energy to reach its eponymous market, but ended life in 1967 when Hulton's was swallowed up by Odhams on the way to being part of today's IPC. At its death, *Housewife* still maintained a circulation of 136,000. Its skeleton remains in *Ideal Home*.

The war made a very fitting, if tragic, division in the life story of the women's magazines. Obviously it provided a long publishing hiatus which witnessed the death of many pre-war titles; paper rationing halted the development of those titles which were still profitable and relevant. *Good Housekeeping*, for instance, moved to Wales (to Hearst Castle, bought with the early profits of the magazine) to continue editing and publishing without being bombed. They soon returned to London, but the magazine like all its competitors dropped its paging considerably over the next five years and changed its format three times to keep the meagre paging up. The last year of the war saw it publishing in pocket-size.

There is no doubt that the editorial standards of many of the magazines that survived the war were emphatically superior in post-war times to pre-war. The whole business had had to tighten up during the war, and many magazines failed to survive. The ones that did still had a period of austerity and rationing to get through for the rest of the 1940s and the early 1950s. The future was to see fierce competition for new editorial products and a concentration of publishing power in fewer corporate hands. There would be many deaths and mergers and competition from the new electronic media.

The effect of the war on the industry was therefore wide-reaching. Before the war, there had been a clutter of titles, many with ephemeral promise. The old letterpress magazines looked cheap and could in no way compete with the flashier photogravure for the weekly titles. Some were exhausted, running features and stories that belonged to the 1920s rather than the early 1950s. The readerships, too, were getting more sophisticated and more experienced, and they naturally began to reject the second-rate, demanding higher quality.

Four

1939–1958

The Government's wartime paper-rationing system froze the industry. Magazines initially operated on pre-war usage, but paper was further curtailed as the war progressed. Many magazines gave up in the bleak early days, and those that struggled on had no freedom to expand or develop. New magazines were out of the question, as they could not receive a paper allocation. Some of the existing titles chose to streamline their formats, some to cut the number of pages. But circulation was no longer a problem, as every single copy of every popular magazine was grabbed off the bookstalls, just as the newspapers always sold out. Reading matter became scarcer as the war progressed, and with the growth of train travel, the desire to buy magazines, newspapers and books was intense. Lending libraries boomed as never before, not only the public libraries but the commercial ventures like Boots, W.H. Smith and Salmon & Gluckstein. The latter was a chain owned by J. Lyons, the caterers, and every volume in their libraries was covered in the identical mock lizard skin. Every major high street branch of Boots and W.H. Smith had a library upstairs but their books cost twopence a week to borrow, plus a subscription, as against the free service of the public libraries.

Advertising space also became a scarce commodity. With their small issues, newspapers and magazines could only accept small advertisements and strictly rationed those. The magazines carried very few full pages and were expected to give priority to Government advertising campaigns placed by the Ministry of Food, the Ministry of Fuel & Power, the Board of Trade, the National Savings Committee and Services recruitment. Women were so often the target audience for these campaigns because of their life on the home front, using salvage, making meals out of very little and the expectation that they would 'make do and mend'. Whenever a woman picked up her wartime magazine her conscience must have been pricked. Every few pages of her favourite magazine gave her food for thought. The ATS or the WAAF needed her to become a cook and they would be prepared to pay her two shillings a day. The Ministry of Food was always banging on about such culinary inventions as Viennese fish cakes (potatoes, dried egg and anchovy essence), cod pancakes, whale meat, Christmas pudding without eggs and a turkey substitute called braised stuffed veal bird. Their *pièce de résistance* was the ubiquitous dried egg, a name which still induces a gastronomic shudder in a whole generation. Readers were also beseeched to save money by an unpleasant character called the Squander Bug. They were generally hectored about the immunization of their children, doing war work, becoming blood donors, serving as clippies on the buses or caring for their clothes to save coupons.

Even if they turned to the few commercial advertisements decorating the pages of their magazine they would often find a plea to use less of the product they usually bought or even an apology for the complete absence of some other product until after the war.

And the editorial pages kept up the pressure. Cover girls were frequently in uniform, the cookery pages maintained the economy theme and the home hints encouraged women to save materials and to dig for victory. Some magazines ran nagging admonishments at the foot of each page: 'Make "Every paper scrap is worth a banknote"; 'Make "Digging, reaping, saving" your gardening motto'; 'A darn is a badge of loyalty today', 'Carry your shopping – transport takes precious petrol', 'Ransack the house for rubber'; 'Be British to the bone and save your bones', and so on. These messages were addressed to the harrassed housewife, whose husband was probably in the desert or on the high seas, and whose saucepans had probably been collected to make Spitfires, her garden railings to make a bit of a battleship.

It was time for the women's magazines to get behind the war effort and to stimulate their readers on the home front, doing war work or in the Services. The irony was that so few titles had managed to survive and those that had were so curtailed in their paging that they could only just carry on with their minimalist editorial. But carry on they did. The editor of *Woman* (destined to become the most famous and eminent of the postwar editors) advised the War Office on how women could best contribute to the war effort. The Good Housekeeping Institute was instrumental in preparing recipes and leaflets for the Ministry of Food; they also set up a new cookery school and a meals centre in Victoria. These were all patriotic actions which probably helped their paper rationing quotas.

By the end of 1942 just about every food commodity was rationed, save for fruit, vegetables and poultry. The year 1940 had seen meat, bacon, butter and sugar rationing introduced, followed in 1941 with cheese, eggs and preserves. Then came dried and canned fruit, breakfast cereals, biscuits, sweets, treacle and soap. Exotic fruits disappeared – a lemon was a rare sighting and bananas were not to reappear until 1946. Clothes rationing had begun in June 1941.

The magazines could only concentrate on the war on the home front. Fiction was very popular but most of the editorial was obsessed with the eternal shortages – food, clothes, fuel, time. Cookery features could only be makeshift and fashion pages utilitarian. Most unrationed goods were 'under the counter'. *Ideal Home* ran a feature on rebuilding a bombed house and set up a 'Better Housekeeping' section giving practical advice for the war-torn householder.

Each magazine tackled the war in its own style. *Mother & Home* in 1939 quickly recognized that 'the last war was a soldier's war. This one is everybody's'. *Weldon's Ladies' Journal* adopted a politician-like, almost Churchillian, pose: 'We are only at the beginning... but I want to assure you that *Weldon's Ladies' Journal* will set itself to help the women of this country whether their jobs are at home or afield, to keep a cheerful heart and to maintain a calm competence.' The other monthlies showed the same sort of determination in the face of adversity.

The weeklies, with their comparatively short lead times, were more topical, and covered all the wartime problems: evacuees, the black-out, bombing, rationing, the split-up of families, even bereavement. *Modern Woman* suggested a novel Christmas present – a bullet-proof waistcoat, and *Woman's Own* gave very practical advice for the office girl: 'A capable secretary nowadays knows just how to deal with incendiary bombs, the exact position of water, gas and electricity mains and keeps a couple of candles in her desk against emergencies, and carries a small first-aid outfit in her handbag as well as her powder and make-up.' *Modern Woman*, *Mother & Home*, *Everywoman*, *Woman* and *Woman's Own* all devoted themselves to the minutae of home life during the Blitz and the doodle-bugs, with practical help for making life better and more comfortable in the shelters, as well as recipes and cookery suggestions for the meagre rations. *Home & Country* was always interested in the progress of evacuees, a fact of life for so many of their Women's Institute members. Under 'Evacuee Notes' they recorded: 'London children evacuated to Norfolk are reported to have put on half a stone in weight in a week.' And they took a futuristic note: 'Hundreds of fathers and mothers from the evacuation areas are visiting their children in the reception districts – by train, bus, car and bicycle. Will the social upheaval, one wonders, be the beginning of a serious back-to-the-land movement?' They could not resist quoting *The Countryman's* comment: 'When the members of the Women's Institute were asked what they found most disagreeable in present war conditions someone called out "Mending evacuee's trousers!"'

The Queen had seen the war out with its customary *sang froid*. Its watchful eye on the upper classes was always evident, and its response to the end of the war was to count the aristocracy's deaths on active service.

The immediate post-war period was not notable for expansion in women's magazines. In 1946 there were about twenty-five to thirty weekly or monthly magazines on the market. Paper was still in extremely short supply and a pall of economy and shortages hung over the country. Younger readers may not realize that total rationing did not end until 1954, and even in 1952 the cheese ration was cut to one ounce per week. Dior launched his New Look in 1947, but clothes were still 'on coupons' and you needed fourteen of them to buy a dress, however long the hem-line. The Government became concerned – they asked women to avoid the trend to longer skirts to save cloth.

The event that was to have a fundamental and seminal influence on women's magazines over the future years was the wedding of Princess Elizabeth to Philip Mountbatten in 1947. This was a fairy-tale romance and the royal wedding was the first bright and colourful celebration in the immediate post-war years. In the midst of austerity and the shortages and the bomb-damaged cities came this glittering festivity. The royal family had never been so popular and so adulated. The people of Britain had shared the rigours of the war and the Blitz with the King and Queen, who had never left London, even at the height of the bombing. Their eldest daughter had served in the ATS and here she was getting married to a royal prince. The wedding, and the birth of the children, began the popular magazines' love affair with the royals. A new industry was created, and it saturated the magazines for decades with photographs and text about every aspect of the royal family. Both editors and readers had an insatiable appetite for the subject. A small spanner was thrown into the royals industry when Crawfie published her inside-the-palace story in *Woman's Own* in the fifties, but this was a mere hiccup in the continuing saga of Liz, Phil and the kids. It is interesting to speculate on the direction in which some of the popular magazines would have gone in the post-war years if King Edward VIII had not abdicated in 1936, and had reigned childless to a ripe old age.

The first recorded post-war launch, *Mayfair*, came from a company called Spry. In the event, *Mayfair* survived only until 1950. But the first major launch, *Vanity Fair*, came in 1949 from the National Magazine Company. The title, *Vanity Fair*, was still retained within *Harper's Bazaar*. But the new *Vanity Fair* created an entirely new ambience, and can claim with some justification to have been the first genuine fashion magazine for young women. The front cover carried the slogan 'For the Younger Smarter Woman', and inside on printed photogravure, the magazine carried page after page of fashion editorial and advertising. The 'teenager' was still a decade away from being invented, and the models in *Vanity Fair* rather resembled their mothers when a bit younger. They were immaculately coiffured, usually wore hats and gloves and adopted stilted and uncomfortable poses. All the editorial pictures of well-groomed, well-dressed young ladies were supported by advertising from a nostalgic parade of Great Marlborough Street companies: Windsmoor, Dereta, Jacqmar, Horrockses, Tootal, Hebe, Bickler, Rembrandt and other fashion icons of the day. It was all a far cry from the glossy up-market world of *Vogue* and *Harper's* and their older, affluent clientele. *Vanity Fair* was for the girl next door, a monthly shrine to her wardrobe and beauty regime. Here were clothes that she could afford and copy, expressly made for her age group.

The magazine was expertly edited by Phyllis Bailey, a post she held for a couple of decades. It was perhaps symbolic for her readership that three years after the magazine's launch Princess Elizabeth suddenly became Queen at the age of twenty-six – more or less *Vanity Fair*'s median age. The editor managed to draw a stern exemplar at the time of the accession in 1952:

TO OUR NEW QUEEN

Whilst the hearts of the nation go out in love and loyalty to our new Queen, it is naturally to the younger woman that she will have an especial appeal, set an especial example. Queen Elizabeth II, still in her first radiant youth, embodies all the qualities of gracious, lovely womanhood.

If the new Elizabethan era is to prove the long hoped-for renaissance we dream of, and England, ruled once more by a Queen, is to recover her happiness, it can only be, surely, if each one of us makes a real contribution towards this rebirth for which we long so much and towards which we do all too little. It depends on us, not on the magic of names, that the reign of Elizabeth II will be as glorious as that of her famous forbear.

By the mid-fifties the mood of the magazine had become more relaxed and more commercial. A *Vanity Fair* Beauty Club was launched with a subscription of five shillings a year: 'Our aim as a magazine has always been to help you find the chic-est clothes at the price you want... and then show you how to pick up the right make-up, accessories, hair-style, to make the very best of your looks, your personality.'

The magazine certainly tried to do that. The city streets of the 1950s were thronged with *Vanity Fair* faces and hair-styles, women dressed in chic *Vanity Fair* clothes, and many carried models' beauty cases, hoping to be mistaken for the real thing. The year 1954 brought what may have been the first magazine attempt to find an eponymous and typical reader:

YOUR CHANCE TO BE MISS VANITY FAIR

There's something about her, you can always tell the girl who buys *Vanity Fair*.... We are looking for the perfect Miss *Vanity Fair*, the girl who lives on a budget but appreciates clothes, understands the tricks of grooming. Knows that these two qualities can give her poise. Where are we going to look for her... at the smart holiday-on-a-budget places now. Billy Butlin, that wizard who can conjure sunshine, sea breezes and other ingredients into the sort of holiday the younger smarter woman adores (we love his Ocean Hotel at Saltdean, Brighton) tells us that we will find her at one of his Holiday Camps... so we are looking in at Skegness, Filey, Clacton, Ayr and Pwlheli (that lovely place on a mountain-ringed bay)... and, of course, the Ocean Hotel, Saltdean. For twelve weeks from June 19th Miss *Vanity Fair* will be chosen each week in each of these Butlin's Holiday Camps.

So we shall have seventy-two semi-finalists.

If you are a semi-finalist... Billy invites you in October for a week to the Ocean Hotel, Saltdean, and we shall whisk you right from your door... not even your rail fare to worry about. And we shall see that you have ample pin money. Then we shall choose twelve Finalists, who will appear at the Annual Rally in February of Butlin's Campers at the Albert Hall and from these we shall choose Miss *Vanity Fair*. Each finalist will be given a special *Vanity Fair* vanity case as a memento, and there will be numerous other prizes, too.

The perfect Miss *Vanity Fair* will receive a cheque for £50, a new top-to-toe outfit and will be photographed for *Vanity Fair*.

NB – It doesn't matter that you may not have model measurements. We are looking for a chic young woman with personality.

The magazine ran a Stork Club for those modern misses who had taken advantage of the grooming and beauty advice and become modern wives. This was probably a commercial ploy to extend the readership base as readers became older.

The editorial shop and store credits in *Vanity Fair* parade a golden nostalgia: Marshall & Snelgrove, Swan & Edgar, Bourne & Hollingsworth, Peter Robinson, Bon Marché, Robinson & Cleaver, Woollands, Derry & Toms, Galeries Lafayette. *Vanity Fair* was always popular with advertisers, but particularly so during the 1950s and early 1960s due to its targeted readership and concentrated fashion editorial. Advertisers became so plentiful that the magazine increased its frequency to sixteen issues a year. In 1956, circulation peaked at 238,000, and this must be considered its heyday. Such a successful formula could not be left long unchallenged, and Newnes launched *Flair* in 1960 as a direct competitor for the twenties age group. Both titles battled through the 1960s but the formula became dated with the development of more advanced titles. Both *Vanity Fair* and *Flair* were to fail in 1972, the year of *Cosmopolitan*. We cannot entirely put the blame on the newcomer. The two old titles had lost editorial energy, fresh ideas and advertising. Their circulations had sunk to unviable levels.

The National Magazine Company, eager to expand their base, Anglicized another Hearst American title in 1954, when they launched *House Beautiful*. Aimed at the young, practical home-maker, *House Beautiful* merged in 1968 with *Good Housekeeping*. It reappeared in triumphant new guise in the late 1980s.

But National Magazine's creative editorial energy was reserved for 1955 and the arrival of *She*, the big, bouncy scrapbook of a magazine which would play a considerable financial role in the company's future. *She* adopted a format and cover logo reminiscent of the Hulton picture weekly, *Picture Post*. Priced at one shilling, it burst on to the publishing scene with a brio that broke new ground for a women's magazine. It was edited by Joan Werner Laurie, who was considerably assisted by Nancy Spain; both were tragically killed in a private aeroplane crash on their way to the Grand National a few years later.

She set out to be fun – a new idea in magazines for women. It had one simple ambition, to entertain, and was a unique mix of punning headlines, peculiar photographs, jokes, personalities and chumminess, which found an immediate market. On her opening spread, Nancy Spain always reserved a corner for her Royal Stories. Her contribution to the first issue in March 1955 went straight for Prince Charles as rich copy material:

ROYAL PROGRESS REPORT

'Why?' 'How?' 'What?' Aren't these the favourite words of any small boy? And these are the words that ring up and down the warm, red-carpeted corridors of Buckingham Palace when Prince Charles is home. Free to wander around in and out of everybody's office, eager to see what makes everything tick: 'You can always tell when Prince Charles is about,' they say. 'You can hear him for miles.'

Sometimes he settles down with a book. He can read and write very well now (not only in capital letters but in 'fixed' writing) and he can add and subtract fairly large numbers of figures. This spring he moves on to the mysteries of multiplication, division; will also start geography and history, possibly French. Up to now he has stories of people in many lands read out to him by Miss Peebles, his governess. (He is an energetic boy, and she gets a fortnight's holiday quite often, when the Prince is at Balmoral or Sandringham.) Prince Charles adores painting and making pictures with scraps of paper on a black background. 'He has a wonderful sense of observation and a very good memory, and the sort of things he sees on his walks with Miss Peebles... shops and buses and people and birds,' a friend tells me, 'are always cropping up in the pictures he does afterwards. Birds particularly. He knows hundreds of different birds.'

And where does he take these walks? Well, in the woods round Balmoral, Sandringham, Windsor. And, when he's in London, St. James's Park. The Queen wants him to have as 'ordinary' an upbringing as possible. So that little boy in the park that you thought looked awfully like Prince Charles very probably was Prince Charles.

Barbara Cartland contributed a story to the regular strip cartoon, 'The She's of History', which featured Jezebel, Lucrezia Borgia, Catherine the Great, Elizabeth Fry, and Elizabeth Barrett Browning, among others. Another popular feature was 'Millionaire of the Month'; first contributor, Lady Docker. 'Under an English Heaven' was a photo series which ran for many years, unashamedly patriotic unless you happened to be Scots, Irish or Welsh. Denise Robins answered intimate questions 'Straight from the Shoulder', while Ellis Powell (radio's Mrs Dale of the 'Diary') dealt with maternity and childcare problems. The irascible Gilbert Harding was invited to criticize the issue every month, which he sometimes did with asperity. His role was taken over by Dennis Norden after Harding's demise.

Denise Robins survived with *She* right up to the 1970s, even when her column was supplemented by the sexual bluntness of Dr Delvin. In the early days of the magazine she featured famous names such as Sir Malcolm Sargent and Bessie Braddock to answer one of the month's questions.

She covered every topic that could possibly interest the younger, enquiring 1950s woman. Camping, caravanning, photography, DIY, films, etiquette, often using cartoon techniques to educate and entertain. The newly arrived commercial television received plenty of editorial coverage. Nothing was uninteresting to *She*. Quizzes and competitions abounded and they adored personality analysis, always with tongue in cheek. Sometimes they addressed the male reader:

ARE YOU A GORILLA?

You're a gorilla if you barge into bed, lifting the bedclothes as if you were whipping a tarpaulin off a concrete mixer. You're a gorilla if you jump into bed and bounce your wife up to the ceiling. A bed is not a trampoline, Sir, and wives should never be bounced. An action that is unknown (even amongst gorillas) is to get into bed on the side your wife already is. This is a cold night gambit against which the little woman has no defence other than to get into bed last.

The correct way for a husband to get into bed is to tiptoe across the floor humming the latest love lyric, gently lift enough sheet, gently lower his body into bed and gently pull the sheets up under his stubbly beard. He should not spoil it by coughing, scratching, sniffing or chewing nuts.

To read *She* was to share in a bright and breezy monthly whirl through every subject under the sun, with a liberal sprinkling of name-dropping and personalities. After the calamitous deaths of Joan Werner Laurie and Nancy Spain, the editorial was run by the art director, Michael Griffiths, and his wife Pamela Carmichael. Griffiths had been the progenitor of the magazine so there was no change in style or content, although there was a drift towards tits and bums and scatalogical humour. They introduced male semi-nudes, a 'Bodies Beautiful' feature, launched with James Hunt, and continued their parsimonious use of editorial colour. By the 1970s they ran extracts from the Dr David Reuben's book *Everything You Wanted to Know about Sex* and introduced Dr Delvin, who discussed any sexual topic without reservation or modesty, and later educated and titillated with his monthly features, 'Organ of the Month' and 'Position of the Month'.

There was a flurry of launches for adolescents in the middle of the decade. *Marilyn*, *Mirabelle*, *Roxy*, *Valentine* and *Boyfriend* were the fore-runners of the teenage boom of the 1960s. Meanwhile, back at the more mature publishing ranch, the two Big Weeklies approached the zenith of their popularity under their famous editors, Mary Grieve and Jimmy Drawbell. *Woman* had achieved the magic million weekly sale in 1946; it was trebled by the 1960s. *Woman's Own* had survived the war with a circulation at 700,000. Both titles prospered and expanded during the 1950s, with the increasing use of colour and plentiful advertising. Readers seemed to have an insatiable appetite for their formula of practical information and copious fiction; a huge proportion bought both magazines as soon as they hit the bookstalls.

By 1958 their respective publishers, Odhams and Newnes, came to the same conclusion: that the market was capable of further expansion. Both *Woman* and *Woman's Own* bulged with colour advertising and had reached their optimum economic sizes. The solution was to launch two new week-lies, with planned circulations around the one-million mark, to mop up some of the excess advertising. Commercial television had begun in 1955, but was experiencing difficulty with the advertising market. The big na-tional weeklies, *Everybody's*, *Illustrated*, *John Bull* and *Picture Post*, were beginning their decline, due in part to the early impact of television. The big budget colour advertisers were finding limited outlets for their money and, if *Woman* and *Woman's Own* were finding it difficult to accommodate all their requirements, then it must have seemed a sensible publishing strategy to launch new high quality colour weeklies. The new titles would also open up a new media opportunity for the smaller colour advertisers unable to afford the high rates of the Big Two titles.

Newnes launched *Woman's Day* in 1958, priced at a modest fivepence but with only forty-eight pages. Like so many magazines of the time, *Woman's Day* contributed nothing new in editorial content. It was 'mumsy' and predictable, with the usual fiction, a dress pattern service, knitting instructions, family health by Lady Barnett, a personal beauty column, Marguerite Pattern's cookery service (twenty dishes for half a crown) and a smattering of Kathleen Partridge, who told us how to recognize trees, gave some 'Prayers for Little People' and a little homily on the Editor's page in rhyme.

And the inside back cover starred Barbara Cartland as the Agony Aunt, dispensing wisdom and advice in her forthright way:

> We can't bear to say 'I'm sorry, I was wrong'. Not to forgive is to keep a hard core of hatred in one's heart, and hatred ultimately destroys those who feel it. It is a poison, deep, insidious, and deadly. Get rid of it, throw it out. Forgive and forget. You will sacrifice a stupid obstructive pride and find, in consequence, that love is brighter and more wonderful than ever before.

And Lady Violet Bonham Carter, *Good Housekeeping*'s erstwhile thunderer of the interwar years, was back with a personality series, 'The People I Meet'.

Perhaps the problem with *Woman's Day* was that it looked and read like one of the titles from the 1930s. In retrospect, it is difficult to believe that *She* had been launched three years before, with its cheeky, sparky and diverse editorial style, moving the mid-market women's magazine into a new era with its humour and zest for life. By comparison, *Woman's Day* looked drab and old-fashioned and certainly no threat to its commercial sibling publication *Woman's Own*. *Woman's Day* began life with a circulation around the proposed million, but experienced a swift and understandable decline. Newnes decided to withdraw it in 1961, when the sales figure had dropped to 888,000 (a figure that would not be laughed at by today's publishers of weekly magazines). The title was inevitably merged with *Woman's Own*.

Odhams fared better with *Woman's Realm*. Edited by Joyce Ward, the magazine aimed squarely at the domestic audience. It achieved a vigorous 1.3 million weekly sale in the launch year, peaking in 1962 – the year after its rival's demise – with an impressive figure of 1,424,000. Unfortunately, this was the beginning of a slow, steady decline; the magazine reached an all-time low of 362,000 by 1993. It perhaps owes its continuing existence to the gathering of the clans known as IPC, after Odhams, Newnes and Fleetway merged to make an overwhelming force in British consumer publishing. It has served IPC's purpose to market their weeklies as a group, creating a competitive buying strategy. Otherwise there seems little chance that a weekly with such a low circulation figure would still be amongst those present today. Forecasts of its imminent death have been around for years.

The end of the 1950s also saw the gradual descent of the two giant weeklies themselves. They appeared impregnable and omnipotent, with their packed advertising pages and massive circulations. To achieve a 3.2 million weekly sale was an impressive feat on the part of *Woman*, which simply towered over the rest of the market. Mary Grieve was one of the industry's all-time great editors and the magazine, with its carefully chosen team of top journalists (many of whom went on to achieve subsequent successes as editors and authors), was brilliantly illustrated, cleverly written and well researched. Its constant rival, *Woman's Own*, at whose helm the charismatic Jimmy Drawbell was equally adroit, was bright, innovative and entertaining and rewarded Newnes with considerable commercial success. The two big photogravure weeklies dominated the market with their energy and obvious editorial investment. Unlike *She*, they did not set up as iconoclasts, but contented themselves with treading the familiar editorial paths, including the customary departmental features like cookery, knitting, fiction, letters, health and social advice, home furnishing and all the other trappings of the women's magazine developed over the century. But what they did bring to the party was smart writing, brilliant artwork and a considerable amount of colour, in both senses of the word. The magazines were attractively printed, and presented very good value for money. They were fun to be with, providing a 'good read' every week for millions of women.

But the weekly market was not the exclusive domain of the Big Two. *Woman's Weekly*, launched by Amalgamated Press back in 1911, was still a goer. Although it was a drab little publication, with a pink-and-blue cover, it attracted a loyal following. Its post-war circulation of 750,000 slowly and steadily increased to a peak of 1.3 million in the mid 1980s, actually topping *Woman* and *Woman's Own* at that time. *Woman's Weekly*'s editorial approach remained cosy and homely, but readers loved it. In the 1950s, every issue carried a leading article from 'Your Own London Girl', presumably intended to provide an uncharacteristic whiff of sophistication from the capital. D.C. Thomson's *My Weekly* also survived the war, clocking in with a sale of 200,000 in 1946. Today it runs at over double that figure, maintaining its position in the battle of the weeklies from the lofty heights of Dundee. The other main contender was *Woman's Illustrated*, a typical left-over from the 1930s. The editorial mixture, read today, is overwhelmingly familiar territory but it was still selling 670,000 copies weekly when it was merged with *Woman* in 1961.

The last launch of the 1950s was *Woman's Mirror*. It had begun life as a Sunday newspaper in 1956 (*Woman's Sunday Mirror*), but subsequently became a weekly magazine in 1958. The idea of a Sunday paper for women seems a commercial possibility today, particularly with such a targeted readership for advertisers, but it made little progress in the 1950s. Possibly in those days even a Sunday newspaper was expected to carry hard news, whereas Fleet Street today, hopelessly outclassed in the speed of news by the electronic media, has increasingly turned its products into magazines – indeed, your package of Saturday and Sunday papers now comes with a selection of actual magazines accompanying the so-called 'news' papers. Both the daily and the weekend papers carry more and more magazine features, particularly directed at women. This has to be a factor in the sad and steady decline of the women's weeklies over the past three decades – they have simply been editorially usurped by the daily press. But back in the fifties the *Woman's Sunday Mirror* concept failed and the title was adapted into a weekly magazine and later rather notoriously relaunched.

The 1950s, a decade of slow publishing development, saw the launch of eleven women's magazines and a dozen or so deaths. Of the launches, only two survive today: *She* and *Woman's Realm*. Three old Victorian titles received their last rites. The trio of *Home Notes* (1894–1957), *Home Chat* (1895–1958) and *Home Companion* (1897–1956) were period pieces from a bygone age, simply out of sync with the modern homekeeping journals. Another Victorian left-over, *Weldon's Ladies' Journal*, born in 1879, had staggered on to 1954. Newnes put it into *Home* and that title in turn was incorporated into *Homes & Gardens*. A similar fate awaited

Woman's Pictorial, the Amalgamated Press weekly launched after the 1914 war. It simply could not compete with the big weeklies of the 1950s, so they merged it, rather strangely, with *Home Chat*, before closing that title in 1958.

Much earlier, the decade had seen the death of *Woman's Friend*, the 1924 weekly. When it failed to sustain its circulation or attract sufficient advertising, it merged with *Glamour* which, in 1956, disappeared into *Mirabelle*. Other 1950s' deaths were *Modern Home* (1928), which Newnes added in 1951 to *Modern Woman*. *Ladies' Mirror* survived all the way from 1903 to 1954, and *Woman's World* until 1958.

Britannia & Eve, which in the late 1920s had been the flappers' parish magazine, died in 1957. The magazine had changed course considerably during its life, ending as a beauty and fashion title with just a glimpse of the social whirl. The last owner was the Canadian tycoon Roy Thomson as part of his Great Eight group, which included *Tatler*, *Bystander*, *The Sphere* and *Illustrated London News*.

The prospects for launching exciting new women's magazines which would attract a new, segmented audience for advertisers seemed rather bleak at the end of a decade which had seen only two successful new titles. The dominant theme in most of the magazines was still domestic. A girl grew up, had a bit of fun (might even become Miss *Vanity Fair*), then got married and had children. Working mothers were still not the norm, certainly not in the middle classes. Evelyn Home, still answering letters in *Woman's Own*, was still advising that once a woman had a family she was more contented in the home than working outside it. The Perfect Wife was the Perfect Housewife. All the advertising in the popular weeklies assumed that the reader cleaned, sewed, washed and looked after the children. The husband was the provider and came home from the office to dinner and a nice clean house. A glance through the magazines of the day shows fresh-faced, fervent Doris Day look-alikes enthusiastically shining out of nearly every domestic advertisement. And as late as 1958 the Bishop of Woolwich condemned working mothers as 'enemies of working life'.

Cookery and recipes were staple features in every level of the magazines save the top glossies. *Woman* had the 'Wooden Spoon Club' and *Woman's Own* ran a cookery school. *Woman's Weekly* featured 'Cecile's Cookery Class' (a gallic touch perhaps) and the monthlies, led by *Good Housekeeping* and its Institute, constantly published features and sections on home management. Even *The Queen*, at an enormous distance from its servant days, carried a series on 'The Home Today'.

Procuring a husband, rather than emancipation, was still the theme of the younger magazines. A man and children were the aims for the twenty-year-old reader. When *Woman's Own* ran a reader survey, admittedly a rather haphazard affair, to establish the views of the typical young British woman, the favourite pastimes were professed to be dancing, knitting, reading and sewing. Only one third claimed to smoke and half were non-drinkers. Eighty per cent went out with boys and most wanted to travel. *Woman's Own* was delighted to discover that over ninety per cent of their respondents viewed marriage as their final ambition.

We can spot a few markers in the last years of the 1950s which would affect the future women's magazine in some way or another. University entrants had doubled in twenty years, commercial television was taking hold on viewing habits and advertisers' money, the big national weeklies were dying off, obesity was being recognized as a bigger problem for women than malnutrition, the first women peers took their seats in the House of Lords, the BMA issued a statement confirming smoking as the biggest cause of cancer deaths, the Queen brought the débutante system to an end, the Obscene Publications Act defined obscenity for the first time since 1857. The House of Fraser bought Harrods. More and more cars were pouring on to the roads (petrol rationing had been temporarily restored during the 1956 Suez crisis) and parking meters appeared in Mayfair and yellow lines on the streets. Women were not yet seen by the motor-car manufacturers as being directly involved in the process of actually choosing the make or model of the family car, but they might have an opinion about the colour.

Magazine prices were basically too low. Publishers had long relied on advertising for their profits – some eighty per cent of profit was the traditional portion from advertising and magazines kept their cover rates low in order not to threaten their circulations, which were sometimes rather fragile. Lower circulations meant lower advertising income. That the market was still price sensitive was proved by Hulton Press when they increased the cover price of *Picture Post* from fourpence a week to sixpence. The buyers reacted in the obvious way and the price was rapidly restored to the former rate. So magazine publishers had to bite the bullet. In those pre-decimal days a magazine had to cost the price of a single coin, a retailing convenience. This gave plenty of choice with the threepenny bit, sixpence, shilling, florin and half crown. Publishers would move one of these financial steps up the scale. The coming of decimalization in 1971 would prove to be a considerable help in pricing – an advantage publishers were not slow to exploit.

Five

1960–1969

The swinging 1960s was a decade of milestone events. The women's magazine business was also experiencing fundamental changes. The Mirror Group, anxious to expand their interests into magazines, had purchased Amalgamated Press in 1958 and renamed that company Fleetway Publications. The following year, Odhams Press bought Hulton Press and their old Victorian rival George Newnes. Then the Mirror Group snapped up Odhams in 1961, effectively monopolizing the business. Later, when Reed bought the Mirror out of magazines, they formed the International Publishing Corporation – IPC – in 1968, and moved all the constituent parts to King's Reach Tower on the South Bank of the Thames. For a time the monolithic structure was dubbed The Ministry of Magazines. Thus, old rivals like *Woman* and *Woman's Own* found themselves under a common ownership. Throughout the sixties they considered themselves firm rivals run by two separate companies, albeit in the same building and reporting to the same conglomerate.

The 1960s were a comparatively lively time for magazines; lively, that is, when compared with the two previous decades. Inevitably, there were many deaths as the industry shook itself out and began to prune dead wood and unviable properties. Eleven women's magazines folded in the decade; most were merged into sister publications. To balance the books, fourteen new titles were launched, but seven of them were doomed to die and two of them declined rapidly.

We've seen the chop of *Woman's Day*, *Woman's Illustrated* and *Woman's Companion*. Three monthlies were also doomed: *Woman & Beauty*, *Modern Woman* and *Everywoman*.

Everywoman had been launched in 1934 by Odhams, going into gravure alongside *John Bull* and *Woman* in 1937 in the new Watford printing plant. The circulation had faltered through the post-war period and Odhams went for a relaunch in 1966, presenting the new magazine to the advertising industry as 'Re-designed, Restructured, Re-thought, Re-directed'. Publishing hyperbole came into play when the magazine was extravagantly billed as 'the most exciting modern medium in popular monthly journalism'. The cover logo was truncated to the single letter 'E' – a fatal technique, as publishing history had proved on more than one occasion. Odhams put considerable muscle behind the launch, perhaps to prove that new wine could be poured into old bottles. They pictured the wives of rising young executives with high financial expectations as the magazine's readers. But the relaunch was a failure, and the magazine closed in 1967 with its sales figure at just under 230,000. It was merged into *Woman & Home*.

The year 1967 witnessed the death of another major title. *Housewife* was the pre-war offering from Hulton Press, the private company run by Edward Hulton, whose stable of titles included *Picture Post* and *Farmer's Weekly*. *Housewife*, printed gravure like all its siblings, was a smart, practical title with an obvious readership target. At the end of the war it was selling 250,000 copies every month, running as a direct competitor to *Good Housekeeping* and the other leading domestic titles. Marcus Morris, having established his famous four comics (*Eagle*, *Girl*, *Robin* and *Swift*) for Hulton, took a considerable hand in the running and development of the magazine in the early 1960s. Editor Laurie Purden later moved with Marcus Morris to the National Magazine Company, and took the editorial role at *Good Housekeeping*.

But *Housewife*'s circulation began to decline, perhaps due to a lack of promotion or maybe because Odhams Press, now the owners of Hulton, foresaw a merger with *Ideal Home* as a tidying-up operation. By 1967, sales were down to 136,000, which was not sufficiently attractive to advertisers favoured with other media choices. So Odhams did indeed move *Housewife* into *Ideal Home*, their flagship monthly. It is not without significance that *Family Circle* had meanwhile arrived in the supermarkets, generating a huge sale bang in *Housewife*'s natural territory.

The importance of the IPC mergers at the beginning of the 1960s can hardly be overestimated in the context of the wide media scene. The famous and historic old companies – Newnes, Odhams and Amalgamated Press, absorbing Hulton's along the way – formed a powerful conglomerate of leading titles, which became even stronger after mopping-up and merger operations. On the outside of the giant publishing empire stood National Magazine Company, Condé Nast, Argus Press, D.C. Thomson of Dundee, Thomson International, and a handful of independent publishers. Commercial television had now taken a strong hand but Fleet Street was still riddled with union power and horrific economics. With rationing and 'Utility' a distant memory, there were exciting moves in the fashion world. The women's movement, even in its more muted forms, was gathering pace, and publishers were beginning to talk of the necessity of reaching the 'new woman'. In short, this was the time for women's magazines to take a giant leap forward, to modernize their products and to develop new markets.

IPC commissioned Dr Ernest Dichter, of the Institute of Motivational Research in New York, to report on the future of *Woman's Own* specifically, but in more general terms to examine the development of the women's magazine market in the UK. This was 1964 and the industry was in decline, magazines shedding readers and circulation. The Dichter conclusion was that the magazines were failing to reflect the sweeping social and sexual changes of the 1960s. His prediction was that age and class would matter less in the development of magazines than interest, so magazines would have to create specialized audiences to succeed.

IPC made an important appointment when they brought over Clive Irving from *The Sunday Times* to fill the new role of editorial director of all the corporation's magazines. Armed with the Dichterian philosophy, Irving's task was to create a new generation of magazines that would meet the demands of the emergent audiences athirst for new ideas and thinking. This clearly meant titles that would be light years away from the old letterpress formula of knitting, cooking and problems. Irving's first editorial playground was *Woman's Mirror*, the ailing, erstwhile Sunday newspaper for women, now a weekly magazine. The sales had slipped under a million, a circulation level then considered essential for a viable weekly. Clearly, here was an opportunity for the Dichter-Irving formula to transform a bread and butter recipe into an entirely original and timely product. The 1965 relaunch of *Woman's Mirror* was remarkable and sensational. As Irving wrote in *World's Press News* (later to be known as *Campaign*): 'What is happening to *Woman's Mirror* is a good indication of how we see the future woman's market.' The title went unashamedly for the jugular in a desperate aim to appeal to the thinking, intelligent woman; its stark realism set out to shock and sensationalize. An early issue carried a front cover picture of a foetus, the inside story illustrating the development of the embryo in the mother's womb. The issue was a sell-out within three days – quite a novelty for the struggling journal. The fact that it had been struggling suggests that the magazine was chosen as an experimental exercise for the Irving technique: better to tinker with a title with a dubious future than one of the jewels in the IPC crown like *Woman* or *Woman's Own*. *Woman's Mirror*, in its new radical guise, enjoyed very distinctive art-work – a hallmark of Irving's later, successful creation, *Nova*. Even the logo was dramatically changed, being reduced to the initials *WM*. This was a dangerous technique, as we have seen, but always a tempting one for art directors saddled with a title they disliked. (There has never been a successful transformation of name into initials. Even as late as the 1980s, *House & Garden* in the USA was translated into *HG* by the new editor Anna Wintour. Wintour moved on to *Vogue*, but *HG* ended up in the cemetery.) But the newly modernized *Woman's Mirror* came to a sad end, which was probably inevitable. The whole transformation was a flop. Perhaps the readers were taken too far too quickly, perhaps the circulation figures were wrong for such an editorial revolution. The sales steadily slid, and in the following year, with circulation down to 850,000, the magazine was closed. It was merged into *Woman*. Such a chunk of bonus circulation gave the recipient magazine a burst of new sales but, as history has repeatedly shown, such bonuses are always ephemeral.

Much more successful was the launch of *Nova* in 1965, the first watershed general title for women in post-war years. *Nova* came from Newnes and was boldly and overtly proclaimed to be 'The New Magazine for the New Kind of Woman'. That 'new kind of woman' was designated as intelligent, thinking and worldly. She would be well educated, radical, sceptical and definitely not the typical reader of the women's weeklies, with their mundane concentration on shopping and cooking. The launch was difficult: publicity was rather misguided, the editorial ethos undefined. The launch editor only survived his position for the first two issues; he was quickly succeeded by Dennis Hackett, who moved over from *Queen*.

Britain had never seen a woman's magazine like *Nova*. The art director was Harry Peccinotti, and the outstanding critical success of the magazine was due in no little part to the succession of brilliant covers and inside layouts. *Nova* was quite deliberately gender-ambiguous in its approach, but the archetypal reader, according to an interview with the editor in *World's Press News*, was

Twenty-eight or thirty-eight, single with a job or married with children... a girl with a university degree, or a girl who never took school seriously. The social permutations are endless. What remains constant is that our kind of woman has a wide range of interests, an inquiring mind and an independent outlook – not to mention that her numbers are multiplying.... What is there for women to read? At Newnes we believe that she is hungry for a magazine of her own, one that looks at life from her own attitude and ranges over many interests. *Nova* is not an implied criticism of existing women's magazines, but an assertion of the emergence of readers with new requirements.

Nova was rewarded with a circulation that quickly grew to 150,000, a fitting bonus for a magazine that was truly innovative, bright and exciting. It was brash, intelligent, bold, investigative, iconoclastic and sexy. It looked good and was always fun to read. The photography was stunning, using contemporary stars like Helmut Newton, Terence Donovan and Sarah Moon. Nothing was sacred or considered 'bad taste' to *Nova*. In 1965 they published a feature on childbirth, with vivid close-up photographs of an actual birth. Neither readers nor advertisers were pleased. *Nova*'s treatment of sex was always forthright, particularly for the middle sixties, and they liked to titillate the readers with the suggestion that they were sexy, but (of course) intelligent. A famous cover feature was 'How to undress in front of your husband' and another 'Inside every woman is a stripper longing to get out'. *Nova* loved personalities, preferably with quotable and controversial statements:

Woman is the nigger of the world (*Yoko Ono*)
I know what it is like to be God. I live like a prisoner in my own home. I suffer mentally and physically (*Picasso*)

It's difficult to imagine, with the hindsight of the 1990s, just how sensational and trend-setting *Nova*'s impact was at the time. The monthlies had seen nothing like it before; a gulf loomed between the conventional and hidebound editorial standards of the service magazines and this pushy parvenu. *Nova* played with pictures, layout and typography, giving the format a shot in the arm. The coverage of fashion, initially by the irrepressible Molly Parkin and subsequently by Caroline Baker, was quite unglamorous and uncommercial. *Nova* found a new voice which had its devoted adherents as well as rather shocked opponents. Bluestocking women found a soul mate, a magazine that was neither glossy nor housewifey with a new *Zeitgeist*. They loved the graphics, the daring, the radical cheekiness. *Nova* held up two fingers to everybody: readers, advertisers and competitive magazines. The trendy advertising agencies springing up all over town loved *Nova* – it was their sort of scene. To them it represented the counter-culture, absolutely right for the sixties, when the mood was innovation and enterprise.

Nova was frank, intimate and saucy, breaking the mould of women's monthly magazines and bringing in ideas, and indeed words, which had simply not graced the pages of a woman's magazine before. To those working on other magazines at the time, it was an uncomfortable experience to have a competitor with such fire in its belly. The 150,000 circulation was an impressive achievement for a magazine with *Nova*'s reputation, although there were as many advertisers who were uncomfortable with it (the 'Chairman's wife hates it' syndrome) as those who took its irreverence to their bosoms. It must be remembered that the year before *Nova* had come the *Sunday Times* colour magazine, as innovative and modish to the newspaper business as *Nova* was to the magazine world. So those advertisers out to capture the audiences of Islington, Fulham, and other such trendy outposts of the chattering classes, were delighted to be confronted with this duo of influential innovation. Quality advertisers, even of expensive and luxury goods, began to use *Nova*. The glossies could not match the circulation of this upstart from Newnes. *Vogue* was selling 130,000 copies, *Queen* about 50,000, and *Harper's Bazaar* a mere 40,000.

The agency art directors, in particular, were impressed by *Nova*. They loved to see their clients' artwork in the magazine, a testament to their own skills and cleverness. They used the magazine almost as a dossier for their talents, to impress their clients and to mark their next upward career move. The mid-sixties was also the scene of the great Synthetic Fibre Battle, with huge and prolific campaigns being booked in the ABC1 women's magazines for a range of new advertisers – Bri-Nylon, Terylene, Acrilan, Blue C Nylon and other brands. These new products were seeking magazine homes for their advertising campaigns, with eight-page sections being the norm. The expensive challenge of man-made fibres was answered by the International Wool Secretariat and the Cotton Council, who replied with their own multi-page sections. It was all an advertisement director's dream, a bonanza – and it breathed a much-needed freshness into the up-market women's titles. *Nova*, of course, qualified for its

share of this profitable and extravagant advertising, at a time when advertisement rates were never negotiated. But the fibre bubble burst at the
end of the decade, leaving a void which had a profound effect on the
advertising coffers of the magazines.

Newnes promoted Dennis Hackett, with his considerable talent for innovation, to the position of editorial director of all the women's titles in
the house. His initial task was to examine declining circulation figures for
Woman's Own. He gave it a shot of the high-octane *Nova* treatment, and
one could argue that the revamping of *Woman's Own* was partly responsible for the eventual decline of *Nova*, as it was swift to emulate some of
the style and content of its cheeky younger sister. *Woman's Own* quickly
took up the cudgels for the working wife and developed a considerable
frankness in discussing sexual matters. It must have shocked many of its
traditional older readers with mention of lesbianism, transvestism and mas-
turbation. Although these seem rather overworked editorial topics today,
they must have shocked the audience of 1960s women readers, some of
whom probably referred to their sex lives as 'that department'.

Hackett was succeeded at *Nova* by Peter Crookston from the *Sunday
Times Magazine* and eighteen months later by Gillian Cooke. Cooke retained the pattern of shock tactics in her editorial but the title began to
slide inexorably in circulation, showing a drop in each six-month sales
period. Cooke's rather desperate attempts to shock caused a reaction from
advertisers who took the sliding circulation as a reason to desert the
magazine. One Cooke cover portrayed a woman sitting on the lavatory in
shabby surroundings; another notorious issue attacked the Royal Family,
alienating a further chunk of the readership. In an attempt to halt the
falling sales and keep the magazine viable (although one Newnes executive was quoted as saying the title had never been in profit) the page size
was reduced from the coffee-table format of its launch to A4 size, and
then to A5 pocket-sized. The 1972 launch of British *Cosmopolitan* struck
another blow, and *Nova* finally succumbed in 1975 when the circulation
was down to 86,000. But it had played a seminal role in the history of
women's magazines and lived up to its dictionary definition of a star that
'suddenly flares up with explosive violence'.

A magazine that found itself suddenly nose to nose with *Nova*, competing for trendy advertising and readers, was *Queen* – Samuel Beeton's
brainchild of 1860. *Queen* had survived two world wars and several changes
of ownership, but its great days were still to come. The title had been
purchased in 1957 by Jocelyn Stevens, the nephew of publisher Edward

Hulton. Stevens, whose mother had died in childbirth and left him a very wealthy baby, had been brought up by his uncle, and never doubted that his destiny lay in magazines. He worked at Hulton Press in his early career but on his twenty-fifth birthday, the day his inheritance became due, he went out and bought *The Queen*. The magazine was then a staid society journal but Stevens had positive plans. He brought in his Cambridge friend Mark Boxer, who had also served at Hultons, and took a couple of years assimilating the title before his 'great leap forward'. He dropped the definite article from the title and hired top editorial talent to propel the magazine into an important glossy. With Francis Wyndham, Bea Miller and Quentin Crewe, he set out to transform the dignified old society journal into the parish magazine of the swinging sixties. It was fortuitous that the brash, sharp-edged magazine *Queen* was to become coincided with a decade of glittering and energetic entrepreneurial talent in so many spheres: theatre, music, cinema, retailing, fashion, art, restaurants, property, literature and photography.

Queen reflected this bustling burst of new ideas. Stevens held court with a sparkling pool of editorial talent: Quentin Crewe wrote the uncompromising restaurant reviews; Stirling Moss did the car tests; Clement Freud was 'Mr. Smith', adopting different guises to sell the same items to sniffy shop owners and dealers; Anthony Armstrong-Jones and Patrick Lichfield were regular photographers; Elizabeth Smart wrote the book reviews; Anthony Burgess assessed the new records; Brian Inglis wrote about medicine and Cyril Ray about wine. Joan Price was the beauty editor, Clare Rendelsham ran the fashion and Betty Kenward was the social editor. A constant parade of talent trooped through the editorial doors; everybody wanted to write for *Queen* and all the photographers wanted their pictures to appear in the magazine as an accolade for their portfolios.

Queen was irreverent yet responsible. It was politically aware but always happy to indulge in satire. Rendelsham's fashion pages were authoritative, although the photographs would often offer their own mockery with bizarre backgrounds. *Queen* covered the waterfront and became mandatory fortnightly reading for the beautiful and brilliant people who ran so much of the smart side of London life. You bought *Queen* if you were fashion-conscious: the pages carried the authority of *Vogue* and *Harper's*. You bought *Queen* to be up to date, to be in the know, to be on the inner track. In those heady days of The Beatles, Mary Quant, the King's Road, Nick's Diner and all the other icons, the magazine to be seen with was *Queen*. Advertisers loved it as it reflected the life-style of their affluent customers. The advertising pages were full of jewellers, furriers, restaurants, fashion houses, cars, drinks, stores, fashion accessories, beauty products and travel. The circulation never rose above 50,000 but that mattered little to most of the advertisers. Any larger circulation would have made some of the more illustrious companies worry that the readership was getting diffused. They were after quality, not quantity, and the quality meant money, old as well as new. People were making money, often by their own entrepreneurial skills, and *Queen* was their own magazine.

The magazine was expert at shaking up an editorial cocktail that has often been imitated but never equalled. The blend of social irreverence and sharp political comment appeared alongside high fashion and the recordings of society. Whatever the other editorial activities, there were always the photographs of chinless wonders at point-to-points and dumpy, shiny girls at Queen Charlotte's Ball.

An early coup was the capture of Betty Kenward, who had been writing 'Jennifer's Diary' in the *Tatler*. Stevens wanted Kenward and persuaded her to join his team; the name 'Jennifer's Diary' was her own copyright. He needed the best horoscope feature and so brought in the original Celeste, a name to be used since her death by her protegé Patric Walker. Jocelyn Stevens was mercurial, persuasive and could pay top rates for top talent. He also developed (and loved to encourage) a reputation for an explosive temper, a quicksilver fury which vented itself on helpless staff. The stories are legion of his myriad tempers, when objects (according to the myths) were defenestrated. These incidents were for the most part lovely inventions and the author, in five years of life at Fetter Lane, only saw the occasional telephone fly out of the window – sometimes accompanied by awesome profanity or frenzied tantrum. To this day, the suspicion lingers that acting was one of Jocelyn's frustrated talents and an innate, wicked humour was frequently behind these awe-inspiring and dramatic histrionics.

Bearing in mind the old adage about the heat and the kitchen, staff and contributors spent either momentary spells at *Queen* or long and happy associations, depending on their own abilities, fortunes and temperaments. The result of the rather frequent personnel changes, outside a hard core of long stayers, was a melting-pot of fast-moving, witty, iconoclastic and literate editorial that was head and shoulders over anything else at the time. *Queen* was avant-garde, infuriating, self-congratulatory, erudite, informative, influential – never dull.

During the early successful days of *Nova*, odious comparisons about circulation put considerable advertising pressure on *Queen*. *Queen's* counter-attack was to play the quality card, with more than a hint of snobbery. As Stevens said: '*Queen* readers drive out of Town on Friday evenings. *Nova* readers drive in!' *Queen* also had the topical advantage of publishing fortnightly, the only woman's magazine to do so. In 1963 there was an attempt to go weekly but the sales performance frustrated the experiment.

It all came to an end in 1968 when Stevens was lured away by Max Aitken to become an editorial executive at Beaverbrook Newspapers. One of his conditions of employment was the sale of *Queen* (Max anticipated a mixed loyalty from Stevens, probably correctly) and the magazine was sold to Michael Lewis, a textile tycoon with high social ambitions. Lewis operated the magazine for a couple of years before selling to National Magazines, which incorporated the title into *Harper's Bazaar* to form *Harpers & Queen*.

Harper's Bazaar had not prospered since the war. During the 1950s the title was operated out of Brook Street, away from the National Magazine office, and the staff lived in a hat-and-white-gloves ambience – all very grand, but not very profitable. The fashion voice was in those days authoritative, but the magazine lagged well behind *Vogue* in circulation, advertising and prestige. There were several changes of editor in the sixties, resulting in constant changes of editorial policy. Towards the end of the decade the editorial chair was given to Michael Griffiths and Pamela Carmichael, the ebullient pair who were also editing *She*. But the circulation kept fading away, reaching a rock bottom 37,000. Drastic measures were called for.

The apparent solution was a relaunch – sometimes a euphemism for tinkering around, sometimes a complete catharsis. The latter was needed in the case of *Harper's*, and a new editorial and business team was recruited. The relaunch was handed to Clive Irving, the erstwhile IPC executive who was now a free-lance magazine 'doctor'. Marcus Morris took over the editorship and the new team included Joan Price (*Queen's* beauty editor), Sally Beaumont (later to write successful shopping and bonking novels) and the ubiquitous Molly Parkin as fashion editor via the *Sunday Times*. The launch, in March 1969, was dubbed 'The Return of the Beautiful Magazine'. The accent was on luxury; the covers were laminated and the subscription copies were despatched in cardboard boxes.

As the first issue modestly trumpeted:

David Driver, principal art director for Clive Irving Ltd, has completely reconceived the whole *Harper's Bazaar* look, bringing to the magazine the work of some of England's most talented graphic artists and photographers. We even have a new type-face for our headings, designed by Adrian George, and officially registered as 'Harper's'. Altogether, March *Harper's* is new, and fat (100 pages), thought-provoking and beautiful. We think it's full of beautiful pictures, desirable clothes, and intelligent writing: old-fashioned virtues that we feel justified in boasting about. March *Harper*'s: we're saying it's the return of the beautiful magazine.

As the newly appointed Publisher, my priority was to convince adver-tisers to return to our pages – even if part of that argument was to per-suade them to desert *Queen*. I had been joined at *Harper's* by Terry Mansfield, also from *Queen*, and we maintained strong ties with our erst-while supporters.

That first issue of *Harper's Bazaar* had a certain elegance, although Molly Parkin's fashion pictures, shot by Sarah Moon, caused not a little agitation amongst readers and management. They had a wisp of paedo-philia about them, albeit beautifully photographed. The ensuing rows be-tween Marcus Morris and Parkin, which, according to Molly's 1993 autobiography, were acrimonious and (on her part) profane, led to the obvious conclusion, and she left within months of the relaunch. Her place was taken by Jennifer Hocking who had been at the disastrous flop *Fashion*. Willie Landels, later to be editor of *Harpers & Queen*, also joined at this period – he had originally been at *Queen*, but had moved with Hocking to the aspiring and now defunct *Fashion*.

The magazine made steady progress through the eighteen months of its life span under the relaunch. The portents were good, until Michael Lewis at *Queen* threw in the towel and offered National Magazines his title in return for the printing contract of a merged magazine, an offer swiftly accepted. The first issue of *Harpers & Queen* was published in Novem-ber 1970.

In the meantime, another old glossy was going through a mid-life crisis. *Tatler* had been purchased by Roy Thomson, the Canadian tycoon who owned *The Times* along with the rest of the magazines in the Illustrated Newspapers Group. But life was tough out there for *Tatler*, at the outer edge of *Vogue* and *Queen*. Thomson made a bold, if futile, move by closing *Tatler* and reopening it as *London Life*, a trendy pace-setting weekly full of the buzz of the swinging sixties. The editor was David Puttnam, later to be better known in the film world. Perhaps the product was ahead of its time, a sort of futuristic *Time Out*, but it failed to collect enough readers or advertisers to make the future look attractive. Thomson closed *London Life* but the *Tatler* was later resurrected by the County Illustrated Magazine Group, who restored the old-style cover complete with the Regency fop trademark and advertising on the front cover. Even later, after development by an Australian publisher with Tina Brown as editor, the magazine was to find its way to the doors of Condé Nast.

Back to 1960. The publishing business, its senses ever keen to develop new areas, could hardly ignore the rise of the new phenomenon – 'the teenager'. The post-war bulge of babies were now in this adolescent state, and from now on would be much sought after by manufacturers, advertisers and publishers. The teenage market was energetically stimulated by a survey from a research team at the London Press Exchange, led by Dr Mark Abrams; it highlighted the vast potential of the market and its spending power. Whereas previous generations had passed their adolescent years in a rather confusing no-man's land as 'little adults', with no fashion directed specifically at them, suddenly the world was the adolescent oyster. Abrams defined a teenager as 'a person who is aged thirteen to nineteen unless he or she happens to get married before'. It was claimed that there were 7.5 million people between twelve and twenty-four, and the market was growing. Seemingly overnight, a rich new vein had opened up to be tapped by the enterprising manufacturer. Under the title, 'New survey of £1000 million market throws more light on teenage spending habits', the *World's Press News* stated in their issue of 4 March 1969:

The precious youngster of yesterday has become the precious teenager of today. The old cry of 'What are the youngsters coming to?' has given way to: 'What are the teenagers coming to buy?'

... Altogether there are some seven million teenagers whose spending amounts to something like £3 million a day. The average male spender buys approximately eleven shillings worth of tobacco or cigarettes a week: the girl three shillings and sixpence....

It is estimated that the female teenager, despite her apparent liking for nothing more than black jeans and sweaters, spends six shillings and sixpence in every pound on clothes. The male, according to one research source, often spends more on clothing than his mother and sister put together....

The publishers have not been slow to recognise this new and profitable market. There has been a spate of new weeklies for youngsters, e.g. *Boyfriend*, *Mary*, *Princess* etc. and soon there will be *Date* from the Odhams stable.

These new weeklies are aimed at different sections within the young age-group but the main editorial interests are likely to be music, films, clothes, travel, food and drink.

Incidentally, it appears that the only way to guarantee a successful launch is to give away a disc or picture of the most recent teenage idol with each copy!

This heaven-sent opportunity of a pulsing and spendthrift new market was welcomed with open arms by the publishers. *Vanity Fair* was too 'old' to cash in on the boom but some of the existing titles, although down-market demographically, were eager to exploit the thousands of new potential readers. Fleetway had the 'Romantic Three' of *Roxy*, *Valentine* and *Mirabelle*, all selling respectable weekly numbers. Other 1960s entrants were *Honey*, *19*, *Jackie*, *FAB*, *Petticoat*, *Marty* and *Intro*.

It was Fleetway's *Honey* that was to become a significant player. *Honey* was launched in 1960 with the slogan 'Young, gay and get ahead!' but the circulation was slow to take off. Audrey Slaughter was appointed editor in 1961 and *Honey* became the archetypal teenage monthly magazine, aloof from the transient and ephemeral world of the weeklies so dependent on the shifts and fortunes of pop music and its stars. *Honey* exploited the spending power of the readers and by 1967, when sales had climbed to 210,000, it was able to trumpet that the female 16–24 age group accounted for annual sales of £20 million on cosmetics, £48 million on coats, jackets and suits, £70 million on knitwear and £37 million on footwear. By the mid 1960s, *Honey* boutiques were opened as shops-within-shops in provincial stores and the magazine was riding high. *Honey* was successful for twenty-seven years, finally succumbing in 1987 after a fatal editorial policy change. It was merged in that year into *19*.

The magazine *19* had been launched in 1961 by Newnes to imitate *Honey*. It never achieved the status of *Honey* in its earlier days, but it trod a consistent path and is the only survivor from the teenage euphoria days. Fleetway brought out *Petticoat* in 1966 as the teenage weekly answer to the monthly *Honey*. Audrey Slaughter was editor but the first sales figure of 212,000 was puny for a weekly. Eight months after its launch it received a boost with the inclusion of *Boyfriend* and *Trend*.

Maggie Goodman became editor (she was later to say *Hello!*) and subsequently Terry Hornett. Eventually the magazine was merged into *Hi!* which in turn went into *OK*. It would seem that British publishers are more successful with quality monthly titles for the young rather than the traumatic and fickle world of weeklies.

D.C. Thomson, in Dundee, have always thrown their support behind teenage titles with *Blue Jeans*, *Jackie*, *Patches*, *Red Letter*, *Secrets*, and more recently *Catch* and *Shout*. In 1964 they pioneered the photo-story magazine with *Jackie*, named after Kennedy's wife, who was seen as a powerful role model for girls. *Jackie* became immensely popular, reaching a million readers in the 10–15 year old age group by the end of the decade. It did not survive the sophisticated 1990s when the photo-style was quite outdated.

Constancy was never the name of the game with the teenage girls' magazine market. Many of the titles were merely comics, and most of them depended on the whims, fashions and passions of the pop music world. Titles came and went at bewildering speed through the sixties and seventies, replacement being the art form. The magazines all bore a striking resemblance to each other – the title was everything. The editorial formula could be mixed and stirred, products renamed to catch the latest craze or popstar, but it was never an area for magazines to look beyond a generation, or half a generation, for loyalty or permanence.

The 1960s saw the introduction of a whole new way of magazine marketing: the supermarket magazines. The launch of *Family Circle* in 1964 was a significant breakthrough in distribution: a magazine that could only be bought at the check-out of the local supermarket, and unobtainable at the newsagent. The concept came from America, where Cowles Communications Inc. published their supermarket magazine, also called *Family Circle*. In this country, Sainsbury's had already ventured upon the idea of a house magazine with a quarterly title called *Family*, on sale exclusively at their shops and supermarkets. It was produced by an outside publishing unit and printed by Odhams at Watford. The magazine was not overwhelmingly geared to the Sainsbury's shops, but ran many general editorial features of the conventional housewife monthly. There was, however, a page by 'Sainsbury's counterman', which detailed new products available in the stores. All food credits acknowledged Sainsbury's, but otherwise it was a traditional women's magazine with letters, beauty, fiction and a health section called 'Family Clinic'.

It was the ambitious and innovative Roy Thomson, ever the media opportunist, who realized the enormous potential and advantages to be seized, and the cornucopia of riches to be tapped, in the fast-growing world of supermarket shopping. The new supermarkets were the place to find the housewives and this was where they could be persuaded to buy relevant magazines. He entered the arena with a joint ownership deal of *Family Circle* with Cowles, later buying out of that arrangement. The next step was to negotiate with the supermarkets to supply *Family Circle* exclusively. The initial stumbling block came from Sainsbury's because of their magazine *Family*, but they soon merged their title into *Family Circle*, gaining the special privilege of Sainsbury's supplements within the new magazine. Another existing supermarket title, *Trio*, was also brought into Thomson's new venture.

Family Circle was an immediate success, enjoying the natural growth market of new superstores opening all over the country almost every week. The magazine reached an unheard of circulation of 750,000, becoming the top-selling monthly women's magazine. Distribution was effected by Thomson's own circulation team, responsible for topping up copies in the stores. *Family Circle*'s success was followed in 1967 by the arrival of *Living*, a magazine which set out to editorialize 'life-style' rather than the kitchen.

At its zenith, the circulation of *Family Circle* hit the magic million mark, achieved by the exclusive check-out positions alongside *Living*; no other magazines were allowed on the premises. The product was exactly geared to the supermarket customers, with about a third of the editorial devoted to food and cooking. The deal with the supermarkets was a brilliant Thomsonian move: those high-profile check-outs as against the bulging, overcrowded shelves at the local newsagents and the high street multiples. Advertisers regarded the titles highly, particularly those companies that desired to maintain a strong commercial link with the omnipotent supermarkets. There can be little doubt of the magazines' popularity with the customers, with their accessibility at the final point of sale, to be picked up along with the Polo mints and the chewing gum.

Thomsons enjoyed their monopoly for nearly twenty-five years. The exclusive check-out sites began to be nibbled at by some of the other publishers and Tesco, in particular, took to selling newspapers and magazines from news racks within their stores. Thomsons sold *Family Circle* and *Living* to IPC in March 1988, plainly and correctly anticipating the future and the end of their distribution monopoly. And the whole world of magazine distribution was to change, as we shall see.

But publishing life was going on outside the supermarkets. In 1968 Fleetway decided to launch an onslaught against the well-established and esoteric world of fashion glossies. Their entrant bore the fundamentally obvious title for the genre: *Fashion*. But the *haute-couture* market, as well as middle-class fashion, was well served and dominated by the old trio of glossies: the revivified *Queen* and the two elderly aunts, *Vogue* and *Harper's*. *Vogue*, in particular, was the old dowager, dripping with authority and knowledge, extravagantly supported by advertisers. It was the bible of the fashion business, considered almost as a fashion trade magazine and popular with the clothes-conscious consumer. *Vogue*'s word was law, its edicts handed down season after season from the Hanover Square mount. It thundered out the season's colours, skirt lengths and fabric choices to an obedient and enthusiastic audience of store fashion buyers throughout the land.

The fashion publishing triumvirate was a hard nut to crack for a parvenu fashion aspirant. Not only did *Fashion* need to win the hands of potential readers, and to lure them away from their favourite and established magazine, but the advertisers had to be convinced that the new title would gain that elusive factor in the fashion business: 'authority'. The launch editor, Ailsa Garland, was a widely experienced and popular journalist and Fleetway put enthusiasm and power behind the launch, quite prepared to participate in the expensive promotional and merchandising activities required in the fashion market, including tie-ins with nationwide shops and stores, show-cards, window displays and fashion shows.

The year 1968 was one of advertising plenty and one can understand why Fleetway felt that this publishing market was worth a go. They cast their enviable eyes on the plethora of pages in *Vogue* and the other glossies. But in the event, *Fashion* failed to take off. Anecdotal evidence says that between the editorial and advertisement departments there was a difference of viewpoint about the aims and ambitions of the new title. All advertising targets were achieved for the first six issues. But the readers failed to appear in the hoped-for numbers, and the circulation never rose above the 70,000 level. As is so often the case, the management called for an editorial reshuffle to try to rescue the ailing project. Ailsa Garland was replaced by Joyce Hopkirk and Jennifer Hocking and Willie Landels were recruited from the post-Stevens *Queen*, as fashion editor and art director. But no magic formula would save the title or find enough readers to justify the expenditure. Maybe Fleetway lost their financial nerve at this frustrated attempt to put forward a serious contender in the narrow and arcane world of fashion journalism. With the smug superiority of hindsight, it would seem that 1968 was an opportune time to attempt to expand the fashion magazine market. There were to be good advertising years ahead and in the 1980s, *Elle* successfully slotted into the market. Maybe Fleetway overestimated the available readership or the editorial lacked the zing that *Elle* would later display. Fleetway folded their magazine in 1969, just one year after the launch. It was merged into *Flair*, which was in turn absorbed by *Woman's Journal*.

Odhams in 1968 were still restless for expansion. Their eyes lighted on the bridal market, which had been carefully and systematically nurtured by Condé Nast with their magazine *Brides*, a bi-monthly for affluent brides and their mothers. The magazine dated back to 1955 and its frequency reflected the transient nature of the bridal market. The readers were avid enthusiasts during the marriage preparations, not only for the fashions and the wedding etiquette features but also for editorial about setting up the nuptial home. This provided ample scope for selling advertising to electrical gadget manufacturers, furniture makers, etc. It was a powerful market, and a profitable one, if confined to six issues a year. Condé Nast had followed this policy consistently, with some success.

Odhams decided that there was an opportunity for a bridal title on a much wider scale, employing the power of their *Woman* franchise. Their entrant was *Woman Bride & Home*, a more egalitarian approach to the whole expensive and overpriced wedding industry. They took their new blushing magazine up the aisle and spared no expense in giving it a good send off. But the honeymoon only lasted until 1972, when they decided that this was not after all the market for them. The magazine was sold to (guess who!) Condé Nast, who incorporated it into *Brides*.

The very last magazine shot of the 1960s was fired not by one of the mega publishing corporations, but by a husband and wife team of journalists with a great idea and a shoestring budget. Working from a tiny office over a shop in Redhill, Tom and Audrey Eyton laboured on their brainchild, a slimming magazine – to be called just that. To be accurate, the complete title was *Slimming and Family Nutrition*. Tom Eyton had been a sub-editor on the *Daily Telegraph* and his wife Audrey a writer on *Woman* who had worked on slimming and health topics. Talking to manufacturers, Audrey was told of the lack of a specialized and authoritative magazine in which to advertise their products to a committed audience. The Eytons began *Slimming* with a capital of £2,000 and a total staff of themselves. It was an instant success, the only title catering exclusively for this huge (numerically) market. The magazine ran on strictly ethical lines, bravely refusing advertising that ran contrary to its editorial standards. It quickly gained in stature and reputation, reaching an incredible circulation of 350,000 bi-monthly. Like the bridal market, the slimming field has obvious limitations (if it is not to be diffused) and it is financially sound to fill six issues a year with advertising rather than to spread the butter (or Flora) too thick over twelve.

The Eytons soon identified two aspects of the market that were particularly important to them. Firstly, the peak period for would-be slimmers is immediately after the Christmas break, when the population is sated with food and drink. If you don't get them then, you never will! So the New Year issue of *Slimming* was, ironically, fat and much sought after. And, as Tom Eyton quickly discovered, the Christmas period is particularly difficult for advertisers, so really cheap deals could be negotiated with the television contractors. A double whammy – space at the cheapest when you needed it most! The Eytons' second discovery was that readers not only wanted to *read* about slimming, they wanted to *practise* it. In no time at all they set up Slimming Clubs, which snowballed to four hundred branches with two-hundred-and-fifty group leaders and a full time staff of one-hundred-and-fifty. The prestigious Ragdale Hall served as their flagship slimming and health establishment.

The happy ending to this tale of enterprise, enthusiasm and hard work is that the Eytons were able to sell the magazine, with all the clubs lock, stock and barrel, to Argus Press in 1979 for £3.8 million. The successful performance of genuinely private entrepreneurs in an industry dominated by the big corporations is always a refreshing novelty, not very often manifested.

Needless to say, the rest of the publishing business had attended this success with envy and then emulation. A handful of slimming titles were soon on the market, with varying degrees of success. *Silhouette Slimmer* (1975), *Successful Slimming* (1976), *Weight Watchers* (1977), and *Slimming Naturally* (1978) were the first copy-cats.

The sixties was not the easiest period for women's magazines, with so many stops and starts. But advertising was still garnering full rates and there was no shortage of editorial talent. One of the most successful new women's titles of all time, one with a profound impact on the younger market, was just around the corner, along with political and economic strife, which would also have a significant effect on the business.

Six

1970–1978

Although the 1970s were rife with national troubles, including Mr Heath's otiose three-day week, the Winter of Discontent, the oil crisis, increased IRA terrorism on the mainland and numerous industrial strikes, it was a decade of almost feverish activity for the women's magazine business. Only a couple of existing titles were to fold, while publishers threw in new titles with reckless abandon. It might have been the aforementioned decimalization, giving publishers the opportunity to free themselves from the one-coin handcuff in the midst of the general monetary confusion – or perhaps it was a reaction to the industry's lacklustre performance in the previous few years which spurred them on to create new titles.

The decade witnessed some important moves in Fleet Street. The *Daily Mail* went tabloid in 1971 (spearheading the way for its move towards attracting more women readers with the slogan 'Get your Daily Mail') and the *Daily Sketch* went down the tube. Beaverbrook Newspapers were sold to Trafalgar House and Mr Murdoch got control of London Weekend Television, abandoned because of his newspaper ownership. The magazine *OZ* closed after its lengthy legal problems.

Harpers & Queen was the first publishing event of the seventies. National Magazine Company, having been presented with the virtual gift of *Queen*, seized the opportunity to merge the titles into a significant glossy. As Publisher of *Bazaar*, I was responsible for organizing the amalgamation of these famous old titles. (A bit of magazine trivia for collectors: the original title after the merger had been planned as *Harpers Queen*. But Marcus Morris rightly pointed out that the new magazine was to be truly *Harper's* and *Queen*, hence the subsequent ampersand.)

The last issue of *Queen* in late October 1970 carried a black front cover and even bore a strategic subscription advertisement for *Vogue*. The magazine's frontispiece carried this black-bordered message to the stunned social world:

EDITORIAL

The first issue of '*Queen*, the Ladies Journal and Court Circular,' was launched by Samuel Beeton in September 1861. Beeton aimed for the wide and wealthy readership of Victorian society, who established a circulation of 10,000 during the first year – one fourth of this, the last independent issue.

Queen Victoria, who sanctioned the title of Beeton's new journal, corrected the first proofs with an authoritative knowledge of society that no editor dared question. The 109 years of *Queen*'s existence have borne several proprietors and many editors. Throughout, the magazine has managed to retain a constant and provocative source of interest – by turns preposterous, indignant, pompous, eccentric, always individual. Yet the skill of remaining endearingly eccentric is one of the many qualities that has ensured *Queen*'s survival for over a century.

During its glossy history the magazine has undergone several dramatic changes; keeping pace with the years has challenged its continued survival as never before. While a steady readership has been maintained, the cost of production, the huge competition from other media plus the uncertain revenue from advertising have seriously threatened our existence. In 1970 the luxury of independence is a rare and expensive commodity.

And so, in the endeavour to keep afloat, the publishers have decided to merge with *Harper's Bazaar*, a publication of the National Magazine Company. The first issue of the new magazine *Harpers & Queen* will appear on October 29th.

During 1971 *Harpers & Queen* will be published monthly, with an extra mid-monthly issue in March, April, October and November. The price will be six shillings.

Samuel Beeton started a great and very English magazine that came to be respected for its style and high standard of journalism, a standard which we are confident will continue. This is not the end.

Not even the beginning of the end, but merely the end of the beginning.

So the grand old lady did not die. but went for an honourable marriage. The erratic frequency was occasioned by the difficulty of merging a fort-nightly title with a monthly. And as *Vogue* was already publishing sixteen issues a year it seemed a strategic course to follow. In the event, advertising became a scarcer commodity in the early 1970s; both magazines found sixteen issues difficult to sell profitably and both withdrew to the more traditional twelve.

It was the year 1972 that saw the launch of the most successful new title since the war, and arguably the most successful and sensational launch of any women's magazine ever. *Cosmopolitan* was the Hearst Corporation's second oldest magazine in the USA, the first being *Motor*. *Cosmopolitan* had been launched in New York in 1886 by Schlick & Field of Rochester, who sold it on to Hearst in 1889 for $400,000. Hearst's ambition was to make it America's national magazine and within one year of his ownership the circulation had reached one million. The magazine was a serious attempt at presenting international literature to the American public, publishing articles and stories by Kipling, Shaw, Churchill, Einstein, Galsworthy, H.G. Wells and F.D. Roosevelt. *Cosmopolitan* published the first stories by P.G. Wodehouse to appear in the States, responsible for his subsequent success there. The magazine survived the war years principally as a fiction title, but by the early 1960s its circulation and popularity were drooping. *Cosmopolitan*'s salvation, leading to the immense and profitable revivification, came when Helen Gurley Brown, erstwhile advertising copywriter, wrote her overnight bestseller, 'Sex and the Single Girl'. Brown envisaged a new type of women's magazine based on the philosophy of her book. She envisaged herself as the elder sister from Little Rock, Arkansas, who could advise girls on how to get the best from their lives, how to improve themselves and their careers and how to live their own lives – not through a man. The liberated Cosmopolitan Girl would be attractive to men, hold down an exciting job, look great and have a wonderful sex life.

Hearst saw a golden opportunity. Here was a bright, articulate, exciting new editor with celebrity status and a bestselling book to back her ideas. They rejected her notion of setting up a new magazine with all the attendant costs and capital risks, shrewdly suggesting she could take over the ailing and obsolescent *Cosmopolitan* and pump her ideas and enthusiasm into the magazine. They gave her a free hand – they had little to lose. If the innovation failed they would close the magazine, due anyway for the Big Heave.

But *Cosmopolitan* did not fail: it was a roaring success. Brown's first issue sold a million copies. (The stagnant previous figure was down to 600,000.) Within ten years that circulation was destined to climb to 2,500,000. A bold step, alien to the American publishing industry, was virtually to avoid subscription sales and go for growth on the bookstalls. They achieved a single copy sale of ninety-three per cent, quite unheard of in a country where the postal subscription is paramount to success. The overwhelming success of the magazine was undoubtedly due to the persona of Helen Gurley Brown and her dedicated belief that 'out there' were millions of girls looking for self-improvement, self-confidence, interesting employment, good relations with a man and a better sex life. Topics were discussed with a frankness and an intimacy unknown in American women's magazines at that time. The formula has been imitated and assaulted on both sides of the Atlantic ever since, but *Cosmo* was the pioneer that became the benchmark for many liberal-minded magazines. The title has made billions of dollars for the Hearst Corporation over the years and it was no surprise that they would look towards this country for the feasibility of publishing a British version.

This is where I have to negate the notion that a massive volume of incisive research and mathematics went into the venture for the launch in Britain. The decision to go ahead was emotional, spontaneous, and inspired. In the summer of 1971 I was busy as Publisher of *Harpers & Queen*, which was settling down after the merger, and also *Vanity Fair* – now a problem property, despite our change of editor to Audrey Slaughter. Into my office came our American president of the magazine division, followed by a rather ashen Marcus Morris.

'You're launching *Cosmopolitan* here in March!' boomed the president, a man not to be denied. 'Helen is on the plane over today to tell you all about it.'

Helen Gurley Brown arrived on schedule and at a merry champagne lunch in a private room at the Savoy, the *Cosmopolitan* start button was pushed, giving me the then-customary six months to launch date. During this period we had to appoint an editor and staff, set up the business function and generate the publicity and excitement we felt was necessary to sell this overtly American product to the British reader.

We had three basic problems to solve. Firstly, we had to find an editor who could emulate Helen Gurley Brown's ebullience and charisma, and who could successfully orientate the magazine for the British market. Secondly, the younger market for magazines was pretty sluggish at the beginning of the 1970s and we had to face the possibility that there might not be the space for another title, given the ebbing circulation figures for *Vanity Fair* and *Nova*. Thirdly, and perhaps the most problematical, was the danger that the concept of the Cosmopolitan Girl was a very American phenomenon which might not translate to this country. Would the British reader see herself in the same light as her American counterpart?

These posers had to be answered with haste as we were already under starter's orders from America and there was no going back. We were lucky, or shrewd, to appoint Joyce Hopkirk as editor, then serving as women's editor of the *Sun*. Hopkirk quickly grasped the *Cosmo* concept, which was fortunate as she had to endure wide exposure to the media and the newstrade before and during the launch – a role she was to carry out to perfection with her jaunty Novocastrian personality. We were also convinced that although the market was torpid we could throw *Cosmo* into the ring like a firecracker, and it would explode with a lot of excitement, possibly wiping out some of the opposition. We were happy that Hopkirk would find our own Cosmo Girl, even though she would obviously differ demographically and psychologically from her American sister. Her attitude would be the same, and the editorial ingredients that had made USA *Cosmo* an instant success would also appeal over here. The Cosmo Girl's interests would be mirrored here: careers, men, travel, her body, her sex life, her relationships, fashion, health, food, etc. Home interests would be peripheral, and babies would play no part at all. The magazine would be big on features and fiction; the features would bring a new and candid view on sexual problems and practices.

To say that we ignored reader research for *Cosmopolitan* is not strictly accurate. What we ignored were the findings of the little research we did carry out. Michael Bird, then head of research at National Magazines, remembers the project:

> When *Cosmopolitan* was due to be launched in Britain in 1972, the
> sub-sample approached was ABC1 women 25–40, similar to the profile
> of *Cosmo* readers in America. It seemed reasonable to expect the UK
> version to appeal to similar age and class groups to those who read
> the original US version. The dominant magazine in that segment was
> IPC's *Nova*. When these highly-educated married women, who tended

to be *Guardian* readers in affluent north London suburbs, saw the US version of *Cosmopolitan*, they turned it down, comparing it unfavourably with *Nova*. *Nova* barely sold 150,000, so the prospects for *Cosmo* seemed bleak if one took the research at its face value.

However, as an experiment we conducted news-stand tests with the US *Cosmo* in two very contrasting areas: Epsom (leafy, rich south) and Newcastle-on-Tyne (industrial, working-class north) and were impressed to find that it sold equally well, and in good numbers, though we did not know to whom.

Much more important was the fact that *Cosmo* was needed as National Magazine's replacement for the ailing *Vanity Fair*, its fashion magazine for younger readers, so strategic needs pushed *Cosmo*'s launch ahead regardless. The research was ignored.

After the sensationally successful launch of *Cosmo* in February 1972 the readers turned out to be single women, with the peak reading age being eighteen years, about half the age of the sample of women who had been so dismissive of it. (Class and educational level were much less determinants of readership than being unmarried.)

British women, when interviewed, also told us that they would find it difficult to learn about sex from an American magazine – but would find French or Italian more acceptable!

Two key appointments were made in the autumn of 1971. Brian Begg was appointed to run the public relations campaign and a young and hungry advertising agency called Saatchi & Saatchi to prepare the advertising campaign which would use television heavily. The public relations campaign is still considered to have been the most all-embracing, totally effective ever waged by a new women's magazine. The ball started to roll with a 'Man Alive' programme on BBC2 in December 1971: 'Who's Afraid of Helen Gurley Brown?' This was followed the same evening by Joan Bakewell's 'Late Night Line Up', again devoted to *Cosmopolitan*. From that evening the publicity machine slid into action and never looked back. Every newspaper from that day to the launch featured *Cosmo* stories, considerably enlivened by the editorial decision to publish a photograph of a male nude in the second issue. The press really took this on, and the story ran and ran. Despite denials, the newspapers insisted that the photograph would be full-frontal. It may seem incredible today that a full-frontal nude could cause the publicity storm that it did. But there is no doubt that the press excitement about the nude helped feed the publicity fires for the début of *Cosmopolitan*.

And what a début! The print order of the first issue, ambitiously set at 300,000 after an initial estimate of half that figure, sold out during the first day. The print order for the second issue was increased to 450,000 – and that sold out within two days. And the male nude was exposed, or perhaps not, as something of a non-event. Not only was his knee modestly raised to cover his genitals but even his navel had been brushed out. In the USA, *Cosmopolitan* also ran a male nude in the equivalent issue. Their male nude was Burt Reynolds, reclining on a rug and wearing only a cigar. The picture received a lot of coverage in the British press and to this day I receive arguments that British *Cosmo* ran the Burt Reynolds picture. Actually, our photograph featured the unknown husband of Germaine Greer, run as a sort of anti-feminist in-joke.

The television commercial made by Saatchi & Saatchi ran to an extravagant forty-five seconds and set a new standard in women's magazine advertising. The campaign also ran sixteen sheet-posters in the London Underground and newspaper advertising.

National Magazines and Hearst were delighted at the explosive success of the new magazine. The web-offset printers were unable to cope with the printing and binding of the magazine as print orders consistently exceeded 400,000, so the printing was moved to photogravure in Germany. The first ABC figure was 352,000, rising to nearly 500,000 during the first few years. The circulations of most of *Cosmopolitan*'s competitors also rose during the first few months, evidence that heavy spending on television can stimulate the whole market. Obviously, the staggering success of *Cosmo* hastened the death of *Vanity Fair* and *Flair* and eventually *Nova*, but these departures were inevitable. *Cosmopolitan*'s impact on the women's market was an enormous stimulus, with commercial and editorial echoes since the launch. *Cosmopolitan* today rides high, towering over its opponents with a circulation in excess of 470,000.

Joyce Hopkirk's launch editorship was short-lived as she was seduced by the *Daily Mirror* at the end of 1972. She was succeeded by the fashion and beauty editor Deirdre McSharry. The current editor, Marcelle D'Argy Smith, has brought to the magazine her own style of malapert brio and incisive reporting on current women's issues. Hearst, seeing the world-wide opportunities for extending the *Cosmopolitan* franchise, quickly licensed the title to a string of foreign publishers and today there are twenty-two overseas editions of the magazine.

An inevitable result of *Cosmopolitan*'s success was the fate of National Magazine's *Vanity Fair*. It had always been probable that the magazine would be closed if *Cosmo* was a success and the decision was taken almost as soon as *Cosmo*'s overwhelming success was established. Audrey Slaughter, the tenacious and highly experienced editor of the older title, immediately bid to purchase the title when informed of the closure. Although this was initially agreed verbally with Marcus Morris, the Hearst Corporation ordered a wider search for possible buyers, and IPC ultimately purchased the title for £50,000. They merged it with *Honey*, an amalgamation overtly announced on the front cover of that magazine henceforth.

Audrey Slaughter was livid when her title was sold to *Honey*, the magazine she had edited herself back in its early days. With incredible speed she left National Magazines and launched her own version, *Over 21*, with a publishing date of 27 April. She gathered together a team of erstwhile *Vanity Fair* colleagues and other professional journalists, including the three Shirleys: Green, Conran and Lowe. Her advertising dummy, rushed out to the business, carried this bellicose message:

> Every month, some 97,000 women have been buying *Vanity Fair*.
> Hundreds of thousands more have been reading it. It was their
> choice, their magazine. Now *Vanity Fair* is to be closed, its title
> merged with another, different magazine – *Honey*. Because they
> believe that all those women knew what they wanted in the first
> place, the editor and staff of *Vanity Fair* that was, are producing
> *Over 21* – the magazine for women who prefer to reserve the right to
> choose.

The advertising dummy got even more trenchant:

> Why another women's magazine? Because 97,000 women were
> regularly buying *Vanity Fair* for what it offered – and they're not
> going to find that satisfying mix between the covers of anything else
> on the market. Our brand new magazine is for them. It's also for
> women of the same ilk who want a stimulating, interesting alternative
> to the hectic teenage market (now steadily losing ground) and who
> don't find a diet of sexual hang-ups is necessarily it. *Over 21* is
> going to succeed for some very sound reasons. For a start, Audrey
> Slaughter is editing it. She's the girl who took a floundering *Honey*

and turned it into the success story of the decade, handing it over with a circulation of 237,000 which hasn't been equalled at any time since. She launched *Petticoat*. And, in a handful of issues of *Vanity Fair*, turned a fading old granny into a lively kicking woman with something to say....

At the same time as the closure of *Vanity Fair* and the launch of *Over 21*, IPC decided to merge *Flair* with *Woman's Journal*. *Over 21* went on to moderate, if troubled, success and Slaughter sold the magazine to Spotlight Publications but remained editor. It was eventually to pass away in 1988, after a rather careworn career, when its sales were down to 86,000.

Alongside the 1972 launch of *Cosmopolitan* was that of a very differently orientated magazine. *Spare Rib* was established with the sum of £2000 and described itself as a 'women's liberation magazine'. It was the antithesis of *Cosmopolitan*: unglossy, uncommercial, radical, feminist, political. It carried no mainstream advertising, running instead classified advertising for folk festivals, consciousness-raising groups, political rallies, lesbian events and the like. A typical page of small display advertisements would feature 'feminist' jewellery, shoes made by a women's collective, dungarees, boots and wholefoods. No fragrances, cosmetics or fashion. *Spare Rib* was a magazine with a positive drive and, in comparison to the lively glossy titles from the big, commercial publishers, looked in those early days as if it had been produced in the back street of Tomsk. It never printed more than 20,000 copies, knew its market and enjoyed the iconoclastic, left-wing Greenham Common reputation. The life span of twenty years was a tribute to its uncompromising and honest commitment to the feminist cause.

Spare Rib died in 1993, a loss to the heterogeneous women's publishing scene. The feminist banner has now been picked up by *Everywoman* and *Woman's Review*.

The publishing business is nothing if not imitative, and quick to seize on a new trend. If women wanted to see male nudes, male nudes were what they would get. In the USA, *Playgirl* – the distaff answer to *Playboy* – published untouched full-frontals of male models, complete with all the dangly bits. *Playgirl* decided to publish here but the British girl never took to such overt pictures and the magazine was but a passing, short-lived fancy. Another American magazine was *Viva*, published by Bob Guccione of *Penthouse* fame on both sides of the Atlantic. The fashion editor was Anna Wintour, later to be editor of both British and American

Vogue. W.H. Smith refused to handle a magazine with such overt nudity and the magazine died in 1978. Guccione blamed the prejudicial treatment on the news-stands for the failure, but the advertisers' timidity except for cigarettes and drink, must have contributed.

The year of the watershed Cosmo also witnessed an IPC launch into the moribund weekly market. *Candida* appeared in the autumn but only survived for eight issues. IPC were searching for the more up-market reader and priced the magazine at ten pence as against the eight pence of the existing weeklies; a significant move in what was still a price-sensitive market. Tragedy struck *Candida* with the death of Jean Twiddy, whose editorial brainchild it had been. She became seriously ill during the development stage of the magazine and the enterprise was handed over to Angela Wyatt, then editor of *Woman & Home.* Wyatt had not been involved in the original thinking process behind the title, and this was apparent in her interview in *Campaign* some years later:

> When I came in they told me Jean was going to be away for seven weeks and I was asked to advise and assist. I hadn't a clue what the magazine was about. I kept thinking, well in another week or so Jean will be better and I will be able to ask her more about the magazine.

But Jean Twiddy died tragically of cancer and IPC decided to persist with the launch. The circulation target was a modest 350,000 but the shortfall on this figure must have been significant. Looking back, the first issue was uninspired. The prosaic contents were not in tune with the opening editorial:

> Apart from our title (chosen deliberately to reflect our individualistic intentions) what is going to make *Candida* different from other weekly magazines? Our readers for a start. Most of them will be recruited from those whose tastes in magazine reading are not being met by other publications. (Is this you?) What *Candida* will not have is a predilection for cosiness, romantic fiction, solemnity about sex, self-righteousness about women's lib, trendy page design or an assumption that everyone is a swinging intellectual with life-style and income to match. We shall eschew the little woman syndrome – the promotion of the human female as the terrifyingly efficient hub of the family and nothing else. We are after the balanced view of the life and the interests of today's woman; the kind who are stimulating

company, joyous, interested, vital, intelligent, impatient and
individual....

Phew! This eloquent credo appeared to be distinct from the ensuing
editorial pages. It seemed to be a side-swipe at *Cosmopolitan*, *Queen*,
Nova and *Spare Rib*, and to invent a pattern that was never there. The
title may have been 'chosen deliberately to reflect our individualistic
intentions' (perhaps from George Bernard Shaw's sassy heroine), but it
was also unfortunately the medical name of a yeast-like fungus which
caused thrush in women. Not a good omen, and *Candida* was the perfect
paradigm for setting gargantuan editorial objectives couched in flowery
and ambitious terms, which could only culminate in an anti-climax for the
reader.

Hard on the heels of the *Candida* flop came the next contestant, this
time from the Spotlight subsidiary of Morgan Grampian. *Eve* was launched
on Michaelmas Day in 1973, with a highly ambitious print order of 500,000.
It was aimed at the 18–24 age group and edited by Trudy Culross, herself
only just at the higher edge of that age bracket. The editorial ethos was
specific and convincing:

> The target area represents a generation brought up almost entirely in
> the era of television and an age of peace and plenty. This is a
> generation which is modern, self-sufficient and, above all, demanding.
> *Eve* is for them. It will have a fresh, young approach on all subjects
> under the sun... it will cover all aspects of life. It will contain fact
> and fiction, fashion and beauty, etc. all presented with panache,
> abounding vitality and a touch of spice.

This was a tough ambition and a difficult standard to maintain, even if
enough money was pumped into the title to give it a reasonable chance in
the competitive and volatile market of the early seventies. The cover price
was only eight pence and the first issue sold 350,000 copies, levelling at
about 160,000. But the contents failed to fulfil the whizzy declaration of
the editorial and prosaically covered the same territory as the existing IPC
weeklies. If readers wanted sensation they could turn to *Cosmopolitan*;
if they wanted more security and cosiness then such magazines were
already on the bookstalls. As the circulation slid, the publicity money
was not spent, or available, to keep up the momentum. *Eve* was just
another failure and closed after thirteen issues. It certainly never lived up

to the idealistic hyperbole of its first editorial leader.

And so continued the endless publishing onslaught on the market. A bright attempt, *Looking Good*, was made by Penny Vincenzi, former beauty editor of *Nova*. She saw an opportunity for a magazine entirely devoted to beauty and health, which would be sold only on the counters of chemist shops – a variation of *Family Circle*'s exclusive supermarket distribution. It seemed a good notion, and Boots were immediately enthusiastic. Unfortunately they insisted on the sole rights in the title, an exclusive deal that would eliminate the distribution from any other chemist shop, multiple or independent. Vincenzi must have been tempted by the big deal but the staff at Boots showed little interest in selling the magazine or even displaying it. This apathy led to the death of the magazine within the year.

IPC bounced back again in 1973 with another young magazine, *Look Now*, intended to join *Honey* and *19* in domination of the younger market. The magazine was notable for its method of editorial production, being put together as an editorial package by Terry Hornett, who had left the mother ship IPC to set up Carlton Publishing as an editorial service company. He delivered the product back to IPC, who sold the advertising, printed and distributed the magazine. *Look Now* ran until 1988, when IPC merged it with *19*. Hornett's second launch was an attempt to publish a women's magazine exclusively featuring readers' sexual problems. This was *Personal* in 1974, a cross between *Forum* and *Cosmopolitan* in dealing frankly with intimate problems. Advertising was limited to the three covers but the title, which pocket-sized, failed to make the necessary impact and could not shift *Forum* from its established niche. It died in 1975.

The teenage magazines continued to shove and push their way on and off the market, perhaps the most volatile and inconstant segment of the female magazine scene. IPC and launched *Love Affair* and *Loving Weekly* at the beginning of the decade, followed by *Pink* (1973), *Mates* (1975), *Oh Boy!* (1976), and *My Guy* (1978). They merged *Hi!* into *OK* in 1977 and then *OK* into *Fab 208* later the same year. The caledonian challenge came from D.C. Thomson when they produced *Romeo* in 1974, *Blue Jeans* in 1977 and *Patches* in 1979. If you are in the market for adolescent comics and romantic photostrip, you soon realize that your product is ephemeral and has to capture the mood of an ever-younger audience, full of suppressed (or not) sexuality and acne.

If we are to follow the intricacies of the births, marriages and deaths in the story of women's magazines we should also examine the more complicated issue of abortions. IPC performed three of these in 1974; all planned to make a spring impact. The first, yet another weekly, was called *First Lady*, and it actually got to a first printed issue, but was halted before it was distributed. This was the year of the three-day week and immense national woes and it had to be a disastrous time to pump money into new launches. *First Lady* was 'postponed', never to reappear. A sight of the first issue-that-wasn't prompts one to suggest that it was an unexciting project which had little appeal to advertisers – the withdrawal probably saved IPC from a financial caning. The second abortion was *Duo*, another shot at the young homemaker area, abandoned by *House Beautiful* a few years earlier. (Link House had previously failed with *Inhabit* the year before.) The final IPC withdrawal was a magazine whose title sparkled with originality: *Woman's World*. This was to be a monthly, and it was eventually reincarnated in 1977.

A publishing innovation at the time, although an adaptation of an older idea, was the introduction of give-away magazines. The simple concept is to produce a magazine aimed at a specific target audience, for instance, the younger working girl, and then to give it away at strategic points such as railway and tube stations. The editorial, it has to be said with only a modicum of bias, is not of the highest calibre but the *raison d'être* of the magazine is its pages of classified advertising for jobs, mostly clerical and secretarial, and for cheap flights and holidays. An important factor in the success of these projects is to find the right type of conscientious 'distributor' so that the appropriate recipient is chosen for the magazine, thus establishing the effective target audience for advertising response. Over the years the travelling public have got accustomed to being handed magazines and, perhaps, look forward to receiving them. An early pioneer publisher was Haymarket with *West One*, but it was also an early casualty. The two long stayers are *Girl About Town* and *Ms London*, both successful in attracting advertising which obviously has to 'pull'. The advertising revenue is all: there is no cover price income and the street distributors have to be paid for their weekly stint.

Give-aways come in all shapes and sizes. The first remembered title was *Modern Living with Gas*, posted to all customers of North Thames Gas way back in 1938. Since then there has been an explosion of opportunities. You get given a free magazine on every airline and travelling first-class on inter-city trains. Your bank or finance company probably sends you one, as well as shops and stores. Since 1979 your solicitor, when you complete a house purchase, has possibly presented you with a copy of

Exchange Contracts, full of ideas for spending money when you arrive in your new home. Estate agents run their own titles, pushed through the front doors of their catchment areas. It seems everybody wants to get into magazine publishing.

Publishers have an alternative to closing or merging magazines when they run out of steam. They can relaunch the title, or as it is often euphemistically described these days, 'Reorientate the editorial'. It often fails to work when executed with a great big jolt because the older readers tend to resent the changes to the magazine they have been attached to for many years. It can also be difficult to convince potential new readers that the old title they have been avoiding (or have deserted) has undergone a transformation worthy of their attention and money. The more gradual editorial change is probably the more satisfactory course, like the slow evolution of *Queen* in 1957, when Jocelyn Stevens moved from the prim society journal to the trendy mirror of the sixties in stages, finally making the big leap. All women's magazines have to move with the times (well, most of them!) but the slower option is usually preferable to the Big Relaunch, which startles the readers as well as the horses.

IPC were faced with the possible closure of *Woman's Journal* (born 1927) in 1977. They opted for the Big Change:

> A completely new and dynamic *Woman's Journal* will be appearing on our bookstalls on 21st February. The March issue will be entirely different from the *Woman's Journal* we all know. It is to be expanded into a broader based publication, still with an AB bias but with a much stronger appeal for the much wider audience provided by the C1 readership group. The new *Woman's Journal* will editorially aim for the younger woman who is on the way up, either in her own right or through her husband.

This statement was the advertising industry's notification that the *Journal* would move down-market and down age-group – rather like dressing a dignified old dowager in jeans and T-shirt. It was IPC's last throw of the dice for the fifty-year-old magazine: if it failed it was for the chop. But the salvation came, not from a down-grading of the editorial to fit the proposed advertising profile, but from the appointment of a new editor who was to revive the magazine's fortunes as an up-market, slightly older, glossy magazine. The white knight was Laurie Purden, who moved over from *Good Housekeeping*. She brought an elegance and style to *Woman's*

Journal which saved it from the unceremonious butcher's knife and, at least during her years as editor, brought it into serious competition with the fashion glossies.

The launches of the optimistic seventies went on and on. In 1978 Gemini Publishing impudently brought out a ten-penny tabloid weekly, *Cosmo Girl*, to exploit the classified employment market. As Publisher of *Cosmopolitan* there was no way I could allow such an obvious case of 'usurpation' as for over six years we had been building up the soubriquet 'Cosmo Girl'. Publishers are unable to patent or register a title – it has to be in active use (hence the merging of titles), and the only recourse if your title is being usurped is to go to law and prove the case. The High Court Judge stopped our case in mid-flow as the clearest case of passing off in his experience and Gemini, suitably chastened, were forced to alter the title to *Capital Girl*. They received their come-uppance as the paper was only to last a few issues, probably succumbing to the competition from the give-aways. Gemini had more success with *Parents*, their 1976 purchase of the British franchise of the German magazine *Eltern*. This was a world-wide licensing operation but in this country the publisher went for a sensational approach, with vivid photographs of childbirth, in the search for a high circulation which was never achieved.

A pragmatic bit of publishing came with the arrival of *Home & Freezer Digest*, published as a pocket-sized title (hence the digest connotation) by a new company, British European Associated Publishers. The company was seventy-five per cent owned by the monolithic Dutch VNU and twenty-five per cent by the erstwhile publisher of *Family Circle*, Geoffrey Perry, who was later to sell his stake to the Dutch. The formula of the new title was instantly successful, a low cover price of ten pence appealing to the market of housewives who had bought the new and popular freezers. Here were recipes for this new kitchen appliance as well as more general culinary features. The circulation soared to over 300,000 but slipped back when the cover price necessarily had to rise. The magazine has had a checkered history with several changes of ownership.

With one exception, the rest of the decade's launches fizzled into failures. The Birmingham-based gramophone company BSR turned their hand to publishing by backing the launch of *Prima* in 1976. In no way to be confused with the success of the German magazine in 1987, this *Prima* was a damp squib from the first issue. The editorial was a throwback to the 1950s, with a staid, uninspired list of contents and the old formula of cooking, fashion, beauty and gardening. Being post-*Cosmopolitan*, *Prima* had to throw in a garnish of sex (now *de rigueur*) but its lack of personality led to sudden death the following year. National Magazines also experienced one of their rare failures in 1977 when they purchased *Womancraft*. Crafts are a difficult magazine subject and the broader the scope, the more difficult to succeed. The knitting and sewing magazines seem to satisfy their specialized clientele but the broader editorial canvas from household do-it-yourself to embroidery, from gardening to pottery, appears too diverse for the average reader. There had been such publishing attempts before (*Easy* had failed in the early 1960s, tagged as the 'His and Hers do-it-yourself' magazine) to exploit this diversified approach. National Magazines put a reasonable budget behind their *Womancraft* push, employing Saatchi & Saatchi to use television in an attempt to capitalize on some of the advertising magic they had brought to *Cosmopolitan*. But it was not to be – the circulation reached a respectable 90,000, but this was not in the National Magazine league. Once again they looked for a buyer and once again IPC came to the table, purchasing the title and merging it into their own crafts magazine, *Sewing and Knitting*. Within a year they had rechristened their magazine *Womancraft with Sewing and Knitting* and attempted to broaden the magazine's appeal. The appeal went unheeded and the title died in 1982, with a low sales figure of 65,800.

IPC engineered two more launches in 1977. The first was the previously aborted *Woman's World* and the second a pocket-sized curiosity called *Good Life*. As this was the period of the television sit-com of that name starring Richard Briers and Felicity Kendall and all about self-sufficiency in their Surbiton garden, buyers of the new magazine could be forgiven for believing that the subject matter referred to pig-keeping and vegetable plots. But the magazine was a monthly version of IPC's popular *Woman's Weekly*, an identification prominently displayed on the front cover. It was a bizarre notion that the readers of a particular weekly would also buy a monthly version, however closely linked they might be. The little magazine had big ambitions, going out into the market with a print order of 500,000 backed by an ambivalent television campaign. *Good Life* limped along until it died in 1980 with sales at 190,000. IPC merged it into *Woman & Home*.

Another curiosity was the appearance in 1978 of *Faces*, from Marshall Cavendish, the publisher previously exclusively associated with the successful and specialized art of part-work publishing. *Faces* was a weekly, attempting to emulate the success of *People* in the USA. The launch ran into monumental bad luck. The National Union of Journalist members on the staff went on strike, resulting in the magazine and the company being blacked by SOGAT (then the all-powerful print trade union), which seriously affected the distribution of the first four issues. Equally calamitous was the unfortunate choice of a picture of Prince Edward on their very first cover. The identical photograph was on the cover of that week's *Woman's Realm*. This unlucky double-whammy got the project off to a sluggish start and the publisher's circulation guarantee of 300,000 was never reached by a long chalk. Probably half that number was being sold every week and the magazine closed after only thirteen issues. At the time, we publishing pundits chuckled into our grey beards, assuring ourselves that no weekly magazine based purely on personalities could ever succeed in this country. The population was too small, we muttered, to provide the subject matter and the stories to fill fifty-two issues a year. Pop stars, television soap actors, royalty, a few philandering politicians perhaps, but hardly enough headline superstars or scandal-making miscreants to occupy all those pages. The custard pie was to hit us in 1988 with the launch of the personality-based and benign gossip smash hit called *Hello!*

Life went on as usual in the women's magazines according to the style and content of the titles. *Cosmopolitan* had certainly shaken up the market, both commercially and editorially – a watershed that changed the face of the younger end of the business. Those titles that had not received the poisoned chalice began to take a leaf out of the *Cosmo* book. Keeping up with the Joneses has always been a magazine trait. Sex began to be discussed with increasing frankness. The magazine that seized upon the newly permitted sexual mores with delight and enthusiasm was *She*. Their secret weapon was their new recruit Dr Delvin, a man who called a spade a spade, particularly if it had a sexual connotation. His enthusiasm for the sexual problems of his readers knew no bounds. Of course, not all the women's magazines showed this devotion to the shrine of Venus. The cosy world of teapots, scones and knitting portrayed in D.C. Thomson's *My Weekly* held no truck with Dr Delvin's inventory of the orgasm, clitoris and erections. (Or lack thereof.) Typical of Dundee is this contribution from the letters page of 10 June 1978:

BAGS OF FUN

My gran came to look after my sisters and myself while my mum was in hospital.

One day, coming in from school round about tea-time, we saw my gran snipping the corners of our tea-bags and shaking the tea leaves into the pot.

'What a terrible waste,' we heard her say to herself. 'All that wrapping.'

Gran had never come across tea-bags before and it didn't occur to her that they were meant to be used in their bags. She just couldn't understand why we all burst out laughing.

Miss M.E. Isleworth

And Mrs R.R. of Morayshire:

SETTING THE FUR FLYING

Walking towards the shops the other day, I put up my umbrella to protect me from the drizzle. All of a sudden I felt a great weight thunder down on top of me.

I don't know who was the more surprised – me or the terrified cat who had just made a flying leap off a nearby wall.

Now that saying 'raining cats and dogs' has a new meaning for me. I just hope it's not a great dane which finishes the saying – and me – off!

Dr Delvin would have made fun with prurient jests about flying pussies. His advice was always to the point. He advised his readers that rape was an avoidable situation with a bit of female violence. 'If you are ever attacked by a man with an erect penis simply grasp it as firmly as you can and forcibly rearrange it from twelve o'clock to six o'clock and then run like hell!' He gave a serious reply when asked: 'My husband insists on masturbating in front of me. Is this normal or just because he went to public school?' His advice to a lady with a delicate sexual/social problem is unabashed:

Q.   My husband and I have a super sex life and we both particularly enjoy finding new and exciting ways of love play. I like being kissed 'down below' but I'm wondering if my husband's latest variation on this is OK. He is keen on wine, and the other night decided to try what he called 'combining two great pleasures' by kissing my most intimate parts after first pouring on about half a glass of 1986 Burgundy. Do you approve of this?

A. No, I don't. After all, there are certain standards to be maintained in this age of fast-slipping values, aren't there? The correct year would be a '64, '66 or '67 – or indeed (dare I say it?) a '69.

It is fair to add that, apart from the jokes and jollies, Dr Delvin dispensed pages of sensible advice about pregnancy, abortions, impotence and other medical problems.

The final success of the decade was the arrival of *Company* from National Magazines. The reason for the launch, or perhaps I should say the background to the reason of the launch, is probably unique in the annals of women's magazines. The story stemmed from the militant intransigence of the Government's Prices and Incomes Board in 1972. This tenacious policy forbade companies from increasing the prices of their products, full stop. We had launched *Cosmopolitan* with an advertisement rate based on a possible circulation of 150,000 copies. The soaraway success of the magazine gave us print orders and monthly sales hugely in excess of this figure. All advertisers sagacious enough to book space in the magazine before and just after the launch were buying the bargain of their lives as they were paying for 150,000 guaranteed sales and achieving nearly three times that figure. Naturally, and commercially, we put up the rates to a more applicable pricing. Enter the Prices and Incomes Board who forbade any increase as they had declared 'no price rises'. This was clearly fatuous and we sent Marcus Morris to meet Geoffrey Howe, then the minister responsible for the policy. He was obdurate: no price rise was permissable. Simple examples like selling two pounds of potatoes in a bag instead of one pound and logically charging more were pooh-poohed. The advertisement rate was not to be touched. We put up the rates. Advertisers and their agencies accepted entirely the obvious price hike. They all wanted to advertise in *Cosmopolitan*, the biggest post-war success story. A man from the ministry arrived, threatened death by hanging, drawing and quartering and, even worse, legal action. National Magazines were eventually taken to the High Court, the only case of any company being pilloried with the full force of the law, and duly found guilty as charged. And more: all 'extra' money taken since the rate increases would have to be returned to the advertisers. The agencies were horrified: they had already taken their commission on space that had appeared. National Magazine's lawyers had cautiously asked us to retain all this extra revenue in a kitty in case the law demanded its return.

Gloom all round. Then, as plans were being made to return the money to the reluctant agencies, the man from the ministry appeared back in our offices. Just trying to prove a point, he told us, just seeing the dignity of the law was being upheld. You can charge the extra rates (after all, it was a logical price rise!) and you can keep your kitty.

So it was the kitty that gave us the encouragement to launch *Company* as there was a huge raft of money waiting to be spent. National Magazines were pulled back from the brink, honour was satisfied all round, and in the consequent rejoicing in victory Hearst gave their blessing to the launch of the new magazine with the money they had considered written off.

Company was the first indigenous and entirely original launch from the company since the launch of *She* in 1955, being the brainchild of Maggie Goodman and Joan Barrell, deputy editor and associate publisher of *Cosmopolitan*. Their original version was to be a unisex magazine and they named their project 'Two's Company'. After much management musing the unisex approach was abandoned and the title was reduced to a single word. *Company* had to be steered away from its sister magazine *Cosmopolitan* although it, too, was aimed at the 18–24 age group. *Company* was launched with a lot of the trappings that had been enjoyed by *Cosmo*: heavy PR, extensive trade tours, television and press campaigns. The publicity budget was £450,000 – nearly five times the money spent on its sibling six years earlier, but these were inflationary days. Two advertising slogans were devised by the appointed agency, one of which declared: '*Company*, the new magazine for the girl who likes a lot of action between the covers.' The IBA, the nanny organization that controls commercial television, absolutely banned this suggestive piece, and rather reluctantly agreed on the alternative slogan, 'You can tell a lot about a girl by the Company she keeps.' Those ingenuous days have been overtaken by the widespread use on posters and the press of suggestive double (or single) entendres. 'It' has become almost universal parlance for sexual intercourse by many 'Carry On' advertising whiz kids. But even as far back as 1973, *Girl about Town* was asking the advertising industry: 'Has your secretary been given one lately?'

The first issues of *Company* sold over 300,000, a figure that would see a progressive drop over the years. The magazine is still with us today, having adopted a new persona with a racy, extremely frank and absolutely no-holds-barred concentration on sexual matters.

The launch of *Company* was high risk to National Magazines after their consolidated success of *Cosmopolitan*. If the titles were too close editorially either of the magazines could have been slapped in the circulation belly with a wet fish, giving the opportunity for another publisher to step in between them. Fortunately no other publisher at the time seemed to have the chutzpah or editorial flair to launch a real face-to-face competitor with *Cosmopolitan*. Condé Nast had been contemplating bringing over from the USA their brilliantly edited young women's magazine *Glamour*, but quailed when *Company* was announced, believing that there was no room for yet another title in the field. But National Magazines clung to the theory that 'heavy buyers' of a magazine (i.e., loyal afficionados) could only buy a title once a month however much they loved it. By producing a near-clone (but not too close), they could mop up the heavy users and at the same time find new readers for the new title. *Company* was given a distinct editorial personality of its own but obviously had a sisterly likeness to appeal to the *Cosmo* girls as well.

The decade drew to a close with two non-publishing tycoons wishing to become publishing tycoons. Charles Forte flirted with the business by announcing his intended title, *Panache*, to be edited by Leslie Field. The launch was postponed and later abandoned. Sir James Goldsmith dreamed of a British version of *Time* or *Newsweek* by bringing out his weekly news magazine called *Now!* Circulation was a problem and he was ill-advised to offer advertisers money back if he failed to meet circulation targets, a promise he was obliged to keep before the magazine was closed.

Seven

1982–1988

The 1980s witnessed vibrant activity in women's magazines; over fifty new titles were launched – many to crash-land – and a dramatic, unexpected invasion from Germany kicked the market where it hurt.

The first major magazine launch came from Terry Hornett's Carlton Publishing, which cast an ambitious hat into the monthly ring with *Options*, 'a magazine about choice'. Aimed at the lucrative market of ABC1 women aged twenty-five to forty-four, the magazine was clearly designed to fill a gap between *Cosmopolitan* and *Good Housekeeping*. In other words, when the 'Cosmo girl' got married, had no truck with the single girl relationship problems peddled by *Cosmo*, but was not yet ready for the intense domesticity of *Good Housekeeping*, she would have a new magazine to satisfy her reading demands. In practice, this vacuum-filling role never materialized; the readership profile of the title was nearly identical to *Cosmopolitan*. The first editor, Penny Radford, was quickly replaced by Sally O'Sullivan; the deputy, Linda Kelsey, was destined for *Cosmopolitan* and *She*. The front cover was flagged 'For the Way You Want to Live Now', and the editor laid out her philosophy in words that clearly justified the magazine's title:

> *Options* is for women like you. Busy women with open minds – capable, versatile, knowledgeable, discerning. Women who've worked out their own attitudes for themselves, who don't want to be told how to think, dress or cook, how to arrange their homes or their lives. But who do want all the options, so they're

equipped to make their own decisions. *Options* aims to provide for all the different areas of your life....

Options threw in the lot: health, money, drink and food, legal notes, gardening, medical, children, motoring, horoscopes, collecting, buyers' guide, fashion, beauty, entertaining – the whole paraphernalia of the modern woman's magazine. Although Carlton provided the editorial, IPC sold the advertising and distributed the magazine. The early performance was very satisfactory, with circulation figures over 230,000. The magazine was later brought back into IPC proper after the Carltonian debacle with Riva, and the circulation in the 1990s hovered around 150,000.

My responsibility to keep the records straight forces me to mention a gaggle of unsuccessful titles of this period. Home & Law produced *Homecare* for the Texas shops, the Co-op announced a give-away called *Superstore* and Allders stores published *Reflections*. IPC advised that *Homemaker* would reappear under the innovative title *New Homemaker*, but after a year folded it into their more successful *Practical Householder*. IPC also launched *Photo Secret Love* which lasted for eighteen months before its merger into *Secret Love*. A curiosity called *Curious Woman*, full of lingerie pictures, came and went, as did *Beauty & Skincare*, another frustrated attempt to produce a magazine to be given away only in Boots. It was announced with a breath-taking circulation of 500,000 but after a couple of issues it sank slowly into its boots. Two announced titles never happened: Argus, with *Working Mother*, and Independent Magazines with a *Cosmo* rival to be called *Upfront*.

There were shifting sands with the teenage titles, the customary shuttings and mergings. IPC closed *Pink* and married it with *Mates*. Subsequently they closed *Fab Hits* and *Fab 208* (with distant memories of Radio Luxembourg), merging them into *Oh Boy! Fab Hits* already contained the bodies of *Boyfriend, Intro, Trend, Petticoat, Hi!* and *OK*.

The year 1980 saw the closure of *Sheba*, a glossy aimed at Arab women domiciled here. The editor, Min Hogg, transferred her editorial talents to the newly launched *World of Interiors*, a glossy devoted to up-market and historic houses. The year also witnessed the closure of *Slimming Naturally*, one of *Slimming* magazine's imitators. Newman Turner put the title away for the respectable reason that they had 'insufficient advertising and circulation'. IPC introduced two new weeklies for girls, *Heartbeat* and *Dreamer*, and Link House, never in the mainstream of women's magazines, decided that there was a market for their new *Rio*, directed at the younger segment, with a print run of 260,000. A lot of muscle was put behind the launch, and they signposted the magazine as being for 'girls in the fast lane'. But the circulation and the reader interest quickly slipped back into the slow lane – in one year the sales were down to an unpalatable 80,000. Link House sold to IPC to incorporate into *Hers*. Another attempt at an upbeat young title was *Kim*, then becoming a popular young girl's Christian name. The cover strap-line proclaimed it 'a great magazine for today's girl' and gave away a free Duran Duran poster with the first weekly issue. But this was another venture that came to grief in this fickle end of the market.

IPC Consumer Industries Press saw an opening for a magazine that would appeal to black girls. They launched the curiously named *Black Beauty and Hair* with an initial print ambition of 80,000. The actual title may have confused horse lovers with memories of Anna Sewell, and the circulation settled down at about 18,000. The title was later bought by Hawker Consumer Publications who had faith in a burgeoning market. The magazine has survived into the 1990s with a circulation around 21,000. At the same time, *Hairflair* appeared. It has had several owners but is flying high today with some 56,000 coiffeured buyers.

The reverberations from *Cosmopolitan*'s success in capturing the twenties market were still being felt by IPC in the early 1980s – *Honey* was getting tired and losing circulation. IPC went for the drastic remedy of a relaunch. Twenty-one years after its trend-setting début the title seemed dated and almost patronizing. Clearly Draconian measures would have to be taken if the magazine was to survive the competition from *Cosmo*, *Company*, *Over 21* and IPC's own *19*. So *Honey* was presented with a new logo, it was perfect bound (square-backed instead of the more down-market saddle-stitch) and £150,000 was pumped into a promotional campaign. More significantly, a new editor was appointed – Carol Sarler from the *Sunday Times*. Sarler certainly gave the magazine a harder edge – perhaps too hard for the association of the title. IPC saw the need to broaden the magazine's outlook in tune with the maturing readership. Slightly at variance with this more adult approach was the inclusion of a front cover mount of a bottle of Bristow's shampoo: the cover mount in those days was regarded as either very young or down-market, or both. Typical articles in *Honey* at this time were: 'A disturbing report on the 1500 women locked up in our jails', a profile on Daley Thompson and 'The making of a man: why is male sexuality so precarious? For one man the answer lies in the brutalising process of turning tender boy into macho man'. This was rather heady pseudo-intellectualism for the *Honey* reader and the magazine's categorical front cover strapline 'There is no alternative' failed to prove true – readers turned away from the magazine in search of just that alternative. *Honey* was closed in 1986 with sales at 118,000, and merged into its old rival *19*.

Woman's Realm was revamped in 1982 with £750,000 spent on television and press advertising. The print order was lifted to an optimistic 775,000 and the editorial was described as 'majoring on food and cookery, with a generous helping of cookery pages'. The new editor, Richard Barber, was soon succeeded by Judith Hall, who declared her aim was to reach 'the Oxo Mum, the happy homemaker who wanted a friendly magazine and good value for money'. But the weekly market place is a cruel arena and the later invasion by the Germans considerably altered the readership, circulation and advertising aspirations of the existing weeklies. *Woman's Realm* is still with us but the sales figures have shown a depressing and consistent fall over the years. They are now below the 400,000 level, the lowest circulation of any women's mainstream weekly. Unless help materializes it will be off to the Old Magazine's Home for *Woman's Realm*.

In 1982, Condé Nast, the toffee-nosed publishers of *Vogue* and *House & Garden*, increased their coverage of the rich and fashionable with the purchase of *Tatler* from the Australian Gary Bogard. No purchase price was publicized but Condé Nast were quoted as saying that Bogard 'had a big grin on his face', which suggests he wouldn't have given a XXXX for anything less than he received. The circulation at the time of the purchase was reputed to be as low as 11,000, with many lucrative advertising deals – for the advertiser. But under Tina Brown's talented wing the figure had increased to some 30,000 by the time the new owners took over. Condé Nast has made a significant success of *Tatler*, under the editorships of Brown, Mark Boxer and Jane Proctor. The magazine has reverted to being overtly social, snobbish and not a little iconoclastic about the toffs it records at play and sport. It obviously fits well into the Condé Nast stable of thoroughbred titles.

Minor matters of record in 1982 include the merger of IPC's *Love Affair* into *Loving* and Trust House Forte's purchase of *Food* magazine. Home & Law, the specialist in contract publishing, launched the weirdly named *Fiz* as a bi-monthly to be distributed through the branches of Dorothy Perkins.

Much more significant was 1983's launch of *Just Seventeen* for EMAP, a new fortnightly for its eponymous age group. The magazine owed its invention to David Hepworth, who had already brought success to his publishers with the young title *Smash Hits*. EMAP's entry into the teen-age female market and also the wider field of adult women's titles was significant. EMAP (the acronym for East Midland Allied Press), based in Peterborough, was for many years a successful publisher of regional news-papers. In the 1950s they began to exploit their newsprint printing facili-ties by publishing hobby weeklies in the fishing and motor-cycling fields. Their slow transformation into the major women's magazine publisher of today owes much to the flair and inspiration of Hepworth. *Just Seventeen* was launched as a 45p fortnightly (a popular frequency with EMAP), but has since been promoted to a weekly. The first issue was banded to *Smash Hits*, giving the new title enormous and immediate visibility. The company spent £300,000 on television advertising and the editorial was the customary mix of fashion, problems, pin-ups, make-up and pop music. But the difference to previous teenage icons was the treatment: jazzy graphics, fun layouts and a whole new visual approach for this market. The sales figures were good, reaching 115,000 after seven fortnightly issues. The magazine climbed higher in subsequent years but has settled down to a respectable 220,000, a solid feat for the ten years in this fickle part of the market. When I asked David Hepworth for his views on teenage pub-lishing, and the reason for EMAP's success in an ephemeral market, he told me:

If the last twenty years of teenage magazine publishing have one thing to teach us it's that success tends to lie in recruiting new readers young, and holding on to them as long as possible. The competitors to worry about are rarely those addressing themselves to an older age bracket. *Just Seventeen*'s readers start at the age of thirteen and hang on until they're eighteen and over. While every factor surrounding the title – from the remorselessly advancing age of its most fresh-faced staff to the peer pressure that looms over both writers and readers and the unspoken demands of advertisers – is tending to nudge it up the age/sophistication scale, the editors have to resist these trends and push the magazine younger in order to keep it in the same place. In this sense, it seems that if you take the low ground you have the high ground.

Simultaneously there seems no reason to suppose that the age at which teenage attitudes are formed will not continue to get younger.

It seems likely that tomorrow's teenager will not always be in her teens. This trend is driven by the lowering age of puberty and an increasing sophistication – albeit superficial – imparted by the proliferating mass media.

While TV will continue to treat teenage girls as morons (when it can be bothered to treat them at all) and can only respond late to trends that start in dark corners of the youth subculture, teenage magazines like *Just Seventeen* can take part in the process that TV can only observe. What they must continue to do is to minister to the desire for personality, idiosyncracy, romance and a little judicious rebellion. In this respect they will continue to court controversy by covering the subjects that some adults would rather they be shielded from.

And although we have to accept that we are in an increasingly image-driven society, these publications have a crucial role to play in encouraging the habit of healthy scepticism as well as the habit of reading. The way things are going the latter seems mildly subversive in itself.

It is, incidentally, rewarding to see that after the first decade of publishing, *Just Seventeen* has maintained exactly its readers' median age of seventeen, representing the youngest age level of any of the non-comic titles. By the same token, *19* enjoys a median age of just that.

EMAP followed up the success of *Just Seventeen* by launching *Looks* in 1985, a monthly targeted at the 15–22 age group, with an editorial focus on fashion, beauty and hair. The first pilot issue was distributed free with the 18 September issue of *Just Seventeen*, the piggy-back technique EMAP has always found effective. The company put £500,000 behind the launch and Hepworth predicted that *Look Now*, *Honey*, *19* and *Over 21* would 'be running for cover'. His prescience was one hundred per cent correct. The circulation target of 150,000 has been far exceeded. The emphasis on the average girl's budget was clearly spelt out in the first issue:

LET'S FACE IT. Most magazines' idea of an average girl is someone around five foot ten with skin like porcelain, legs like double yellow lines and a Swiss bank account. And when Ms Average leaves the salon sporting £98 worth of root-permed-highlights and slips into her designer labels, they look terrific.... Just like they did on the catwalk.

Enter *Looks*. A magazine all about fashion, hair and make-up. Here to prove that any girl can look great, regardless of size, shape or salary, without having to diet to distraction or spend a fortune. *Looks* is packed with ideas, advice, inspiration.... *Looks*'ll keep you in touch with the latest from the catwalk to the chemists' shelves....

Yet another bid by EMAP for domination of the younger market came with the launch of *More!* in 1988. *More!*'s original gimmick was to carry a twelve-page fashion fold-out in each fortnightly issue – hence the title. The pilot issue was given away as an extra with *The Mail on Sunday*'s *You* magazine and the first bookstall issue was sold in a plastic cover and contained a bonus fashion guide. The launch brochure explained the editorial ethos to advertisers:

The woman *More!* is aimed at is uneasy with the glossy monthlies, too old for *Just Seventeen* and she feels that the current crop of weaklies (even the new ones) are too 'mumsy'. *More!* will be snappy, easy to read and topical. More importantly, all the editorial will be relevant to the under thirty, independent woman.

The branding and positioning of the magazine were very positive. The circulation director's forecast that *More!* would be the magazine of the 1980s, while *Cosmopolitan* was the magazine of the 1970s, has not quite materialized but *More!* is selling 367,000 copies (the launch guarantee was 225,000) – still 90,000 behind *Cosmo*. Like many magazines in the 1990s, *More!* has moved towards the overt sex feature. In 1993 one issue carried a booklet wrapped in a sort of kitchen foil and entitled 'Men: A User's Guide'. This was a unique insight into 'men's minds and trousers' containing such articles as 'Me and my willy' and such ladylike sentiments as: 'Come to think of it, afternoon shags are a different kettle of fish altogether.' I often contemplate how all the sex instruction, comment, and language in today's young women's magazines would have shocked and baffled the uncouth denizens I lived with in the army nissen hut back in 1945.

We were forewarned. In a 1988 interview in a trade magazine Wendy Bristow, the editor, told us that *More!* would be 'a bit raunchy and unpredictable and sometimes off the wall'. The magazine was for 'Fiona who lives in Fife and works as a secretary and for Tracey who lives in Wigan and works as a hairdresser'. The common ground was their interest in their looks and their attitude to the world. *More!* was clearly for the girl who had outgrown *Just Seventeen* and wanted to move towards more adult entertainment. EMAP were successfully capturing a great deal of the middle ground between the near-comics and the more mature younger titles. They were later to add *Big!* (another fortnightly, another exclamation mark) to their stable, on the way to completing their ambitions to reach the female population from 'ten to thirty'. Eventually, *New Woman* and *Elle* would be added to their impressive collection.

A gallant plunge into the maelstrom came in 1984 when *Working Woman* arrived. The title had done well in the USA with a rapidly ascending circulation reaching 700,000. The American owners were convinced that the UK market would be happy and ready to receive a British version of their magazine and held meetings, which proved fruitless, with all the major publishing companies. But Audrey Slaughter, the editor with *Honey*, *Vanity Fair*, *Over 21* and *Weight Watchers* to her credit, was convinced of the title's potential; she set up a private company with a capital of £600,000. The magazine was launched with a cover price of £1.30, then quite a premium price, and the editorial line was positive, unambivalent and focused on the working world of women. Said Slaughter:

> *Working Woman* is the magazine for women who make things happen. The ones who see themselves as part and parcel of business life, political life, home life. They want a piece of the action and are prepared to make sacrifices to get it – working harder, investing more in their own development and their skills. They've come to terms with the fact that cheap domestic help is no longer theirs for the paying – so they substitute organization and automation. They know that if they have children they will be theirs – on loan – for such a very short time in terms of full care that there's going to be a whole lot of left over life to have.... *Working Woman* is for realists. The women with drive who won't accept limitations, who believe in themselves and their abilities, who are on the move. If a grocer's daughter from Grantham can become Prime Minister, it's all possible!

The magazine was full of role models, financial advice, educational information, suitable working fashion, equal pay studies and sharp comments about unfair treatment of working women. The settle-down circulation was seen as 70,000 and Slaughter, never a lady to mince her words, said that 'the magazine can appeal to the executive woman just as *Cosmo* appeals to the secretary trying to be a p.a. whose idea of success is still marrying respectably'.

Working Woman was given a prominent launch, including poster advertising, and the initial print order was raised to 87,000. But the magazine never got to the heart of its intended readership, or perhaps there were just not enough executive women with the burning ideals and objectives set out by Slaughter in her editorial leader. In the American big cities, those ambitious business women out for personal executive success are dubbed 'pink collar'. Perhaps ten years later the magazine might have been better received, although it is a hard editorial concept. One feels that the successful business woman will read the serious national press, *The Economist* and perhaps a fashion glossy. The less ambitious working woman has a wealth of magazines at her disposal and the business side of her life might come second to home and family life.

Certainly, *Working Woman*'s problems stemmed from a weak circulation rather than the editorial style or content, which was efficient and logical. By 1986 the sales figure was a faltering and pallid 33,000. The magazine had been partly financed by the American instigators, who held a twenty per cent stake. But they pulled out of the British version in 1985 and the magazine was 'rescued' by Peter Cadbury, the millionaire industrialist. Slaughter left after his purchase and the new editor (not laden with experience) declared that the editorial policy had been too strident and too earnest: she would now shift the magazine towards more general features. A new advertising agency was appointed to stimulate the faded circulation. They resorted to a psychographic study which divided women into three broad groups: feminists, feminines (men-orientated) and females, a fluctuation between the other two groups. Then they looked at the strivers, traditionalists (content with themselves and their magazines) and latent strivers, seemingly a rather confused lot. The agency considered that the feminists and strivers were already probably readers of *Working Woman*, while the feminines and traditionalists were not in the catchment group. This conclusion, unfortunately, left them where they had started – with the latent non-strivers and non-readers of women's magazines. Peter Cadbury wisely closed the magazine in 1986 but it was purchased by Preston Publications. The story was a mess of resignations, threats from creditors and general confusion before the title faded away.

The aroma of cooking began to permeate the bookstalls in 1984, the start of a series of attempts to establish the capricious category of foodie magazines. The first and the grandest was IPC's *A la Carte*, directed at the enthusiastic and affluent gourmet who had to fork out a high £1.75 for a copy. Very glossy production and high quality photography inspired a circulation target of 80,000. The sales never reached that figure and the magazine was taken off the stove in 1988. At the same time, Marshall Cavendish went for the big, mass sale when they introduced *Cook's Weekly*, priced at a more humble thirty-five pence. Their ambitions were high, as the first issue was distributed with the 7 November issue of *TV Times* and the Irish *Woman's Way*, achieving a distribution of 3.5 million copies backed with a launch budget of £250,000. The second issue was given an unrealistic print run of 600,000 copies and a declared intention to settle at a minimum of 250,000 copies a week. It could never be. Cookery and food are so comprehensively covered by the women's weeklies that a weekly devoted to the kitchen has little chance to capture such a diverse market economically. *Cook's Weekly* had the gas turned off in 1986, just a couple of years after the extravagant launch. The title was reinstated by Robert Maxwell, sold on to Northern & Shell and later went into the publishing void.

British European Associated Publishers (BEAP), the British end of the Dutch publisher VNU, had launched *Home & Freezer Digest* successfully back in 1972. They now announced a new weekly to be called *What's Cooking*. But when they witnessed the problems of *Cook's Weekly* they realized there was no room for one, never mind two, cooking weeklies, and they cancelled the launch. A BEAP spokesman announced, with an apposite simile, that 'they would hold fire, even if it means getting egg on our faces'.

But Marshall Cavendish were not finished in the kitchen. In 1986 they brought out *Taste*, a bi-monthly glossy. The publishers saw the opportunity of exploiting the meaning of the title by extending it to 'good taste' in travel, leisure and up-market life-style, thus considerably widening their potential trawl for advertising outside the narrower field of cookery and wine. *Taste* was a bold attempt with an initial print run of 145,000. But Marshall Cavendish was now owned by a Singapore company who took the decision to pull out of conventional publishing and stick to their list, namely part-works. So *Taste* was sold to BEAP. The foodie market simmered for a few years until the BBC, via Redwood Publishing, brought out *Good Food* with the controversial backing and overt publicity of the Food Programme. The title was an instant success and probably stirred Grühner & Jahr, now esconced in the UK as we shall see, to launch *Let's Cook*, and Broglia Publishing to launch *What Food*? Both these ventures were short-lived, G & J grumbling, with some justification, at the unfairness of the BBC free publicity. *Taste* is still with us today, after several changes of ownership, and *Home & Freezer Digest* has been transformed into *Home Cooking*, owned by Argus. But the BBC rules the roost with *Good Food* and their later addition of *BBC Vegetarian Good Food*.

The teenage market battled on during the 1980s. Early confusion came from IPC with the announcement of a new title to be called *True Love*, a merger of *True* and *Hers*. But there was trouble at the editorial mill, with journalists disputing a pay claim with the management. The result was a perfunctory cancellation of the proposed merger and the sudden death of both the titles due to be merged. And later in the same year, 1984, IPC merged *Oh Boy!* with *My Guy*, an action that coincided with EMAP's announcement that their roaring success, *Just Seventeen*, would go weekly in the spring of 1985. Two new contenders now appeared on the highly competitive teenage market. First, IPC launched *Mizz*, aimed at the seventeen-year-old girl who maybe wasn't reading *Just Seventeen*. *Mizz* enjoyed a massive launch budget of £650,000 and a marketing controller who excitedly told the trade press:

We have identified a whole new market. These women have become self-aware to the challenge of adulthood. Photolove stories are behind them but they're not ready for home-making, divorce and Greenham Common. It is amongst this age-group that we have found a widespread dissatisfaction with older and younger titles.

So sucks to EMAP and *Cosmopolitan*!

Mizz was a fortnightly with the now-familiar jazzy layouts, but lacking that Hepworth panache. The editor's introduction was terse and just a little short of brassy self-confidence:

Mizz. The new magazine. We won't say it's different, we won't say it's better. We won't even claim it's more colourful and full of things to make your life more fun. But we hope you'll find it all those things and a whole lot more. Every fortnight. PLAY IT LOUD.

Up in Dundee they were at it again. D.C. Thomson came up with the curiously titled *Etcetera,* a forty-pence fortnightly. This was 'the New Magazine for the 80s Girl'. Here we go again:

Welcome to *Etcetera*. A mouth-watering cocktail of fashion, fiction, people and lifestyle is now yours for the taking.... You'll be glad to know that *Etcetera* won't try to pigeon-hole you into the tired old moulds of other magazines. We won't devote ourselves to articles on how to please your man (or even how to grab your guy). Instead, we'll devote ourselves to pleasing you. Which is exactly why *Etcetera* is going to become a habit with you every fortnight from now on.

Caledonian knocking indeed. But the magazine was rather dull, with too much monotone. It was a futile attempt to get trendy. The early print runs were 400,000 but they never saw sales of that calibre. The title was closed the following year, never having disclosed a sales figure. D.C. Thomson, coy as ever, merely said that they had not sold as many copies as they had wanted to.

A different kettle of fish was Thomson's 1989 launch *Catch*, more glossy, more colourful and aimed at the seventeen- to twenty-one-year-old 'ordinary' girl:

> She may be a nurse, secretary, hairdresser, at college or whatever, and her lifestyle is ruled by her cash-flow. . . . She's the girl who saves up for her annual holiday in Benidorm or Ibiza. . . . Her clothes are mainly from the catalogues or chainstores . . . designer labels are out of her league and if she wore some of the outfits she's seen in glossy magazines she'd be too embarrassed to walk down the High Street.

This was the description of the potential reader to the advertiser – without the readers' knowledge. The rather mundane portrait of their average reader is belied by the bright editorial but today, four years after the launch, with a sales figure of just under 100,000, the advertiser is still being told that the target reader is 'an ordinary girl seventeen to twenty-one C1 C2 in full-time education or employment'.

Another type of young woman was being sought by a new title called *Chic*, aimed at young black women, with a cover price of ninety pence and a print run of 30,000 copies – modest but with a naturally restricted target audience. The editorial policy was to cover 'the whole spectrum of hair care and beauty, as well as fashion, films and all the other facets which contribute to the total look of a sophisticated, contemporary black woman'. The competitors were *Root*, and *Black Beauty and Hair*, the publisher of which warned the newcomer that the main problem they would face was distribution. '*Chic* will discover, as we have, that a lot of newsagents simply don't think that a magazine with a black person on the cover will sell.' *Chic* disappeared, but a 1989 attempt on the same market, *Candace*, with a more family-orientated editorial, is still with us, aiming at black women aged between twenty and fifty-five.

The teenage carousel went on whizzing around. IPC relaunched *Girl* in 1988 with a complete editorial overhaul. 'Everything but the title will disappear overnight' as the weekly cast off its down-market comic-strip image to become the 'first proper magazine for ten- to fourteen-year-old girls'. IPC had researched the *Girl* readership and discovered that their teeny-boppers wanted contents changes. 'These girls perceive comic strips as babyish and they don't want that so we are getting rid of them,' said the publisher Bridget LeGood. 'But we will retain one photo story each week.' IPC took the relaunch seriously with a £250,000 TV and poster campaign. In the same year, D.C. Thomson merged *Patches* with *Blue Jeans* and finally *Blue Jeans* with *Jackie*. IPC reduced their weekly *Loving* to a monthly, and merged *Girl's Monthly* into *My Guy Monthly*. By January 1970 the relaunch of *Girl* was clearly a failure and it was merged into *My Guy*. IPC also merged *Photo Loving* into *My Guy Monthly*, and if you can stand this merger mania, D.C. Thomson closed *Secrets* in 1991, merged it with *My Weekly*, and merged *Judy* into *Mandy*.

The homes category, which had seen little development for some years, had a small but expensive stirring in 1985 when IPC went all out with the launch of *In Store*. The magazine was in catalogue style, perhaps encouraged by the bookstall success of the *Habitat* catalogues. The print run of *In Store* was 350,000 and the promotion budget a massive £1.3 million: the heaviest and most expensive for a new magazine at that time. The editorial broke new ground for a conventional homes magazine as the whole title was a review of listings of merchandise available in the shops. As the editor told us:

Trying to see the range of furnishings and accessories available can be a time-consuming job in itself, but trying to track down a particular furniture style or fabric design is often impossible! This is where *In Store* can help, because we'll be taking the searching out of home-making by showing you the goods available and guiding you to where you can buy them. Each month we'll have six or seven merchandise reviews, illustrating a wide range of items in terms of style, price and outlet, so every furnishing taste and budget will be catered for.... Now, instead of spending hours looking round the shops, you can use *In Store* as your shop window to the goods currently available.

On reflection, *In Store* was a capital idea which should have succeeded. The approach was a novel one and there is no doubt that catalogues were becoming popular with the shopping public. IPC certainly had a great deal of faith in the concept: 'People are moving away from general to more specialised publications and there is no other magazine that specialises in the home.' The last remark rang a bit peculiar, coming as it did from the publishers of *Ideal Home* and *Homes & Gardens*! But IPC's confidence shone brightly with their statement that

> there is an increasing tendency for people to set up home before they get married. The home is more of a leisure centre than it used to be and people spend more money on furnishings for their home than ever before. For this reason we feel there will be no problem in sustaining a monthly publication.

The catalogue style was carried throughout the magazine with small two-inch square photographs of the selected merchandise – beds, cutlery, table linen, dining-room furniture and so on.

But the concept never caught on with the public and IPC watched the circulation walk through treacle. The first ABC figure was 116,000 and the next 107,000, a far cry from the bullish launch figure. Advertising, too, was disappointing with only four hundred pages in the first full year instead of the anticipated seven hundred. The revenue was insufficient to maintain and develop the costly editorial and the official obituary read: 'The magazine's narrow editorial base meant that although we were getting most of the major home interest accounts, we couldn't take in broader categories like cars and food. One option considered was to broaden the editorial but then we would have been competing in a very crowded market.' So it was curtains for *In Store*, a very expensive 'miss'. The title was folded into *Ideal Home* and began to appear as an occasional thirty-two page banded supplement to that magazine, but after about a year it was decently buried.

Rupert Murdoch decided to extend his media interests in 1985 with a British launch of the famous and classic French fashion weekly *Elle*. This was a joint publishing venture with the French owners Hachette, who had joined forces with Murdoch to launch the title successfully in the States. *Elle* in France had always been the darling of the fashion editors all over the world, a style catalyst and almost a trendy fashion bible. The British launch was to be a major publishing event, with pilot issues 'tasted' in two editions of the *Sunday Times* colour magazine (May and September). On both occasions *Elle* appeared as a sixty-four page pull-out, backed by prestige international advertisers. The appearance in the middle of the Sunday magazine was explained:

> Over the past forty years *Elle* has become easily the best-known women's magazine in France – developing a lively content and highly unusual style of presentation which is widely admired throughout the world of publishing. Well-established editions in Japanese and Arabic have been followed recently by the successful launch of an English language *Elle* in the United States. And now a new edition is being prepared specially for the British market. . . . We are delighted to play host to a unique publishing experiment and feel confident that *Elle* will rapidly become a firm favourite among the two million readers of the *Sunday Times*.

And to emphasize the efficiency of the test, readers were asked: 'Let us know what you think of the taste of *Elle* – what you don't like as much as you do like, what you would like more of as well as what you can do without.' Joyce Hopkirk, the editorial director, told a trade weekly:

> . . . features on women's orgasms are a bit passé. Women are no longer interested in very wordy, very anxious articles such as are offered in *Cosmopolitan* and *Company* with fashion thrown in. There's a new breed of reader with no special magazine catering for them. This is where *Elle* will succeed. It is primarily a style magazine with words.

This from the woman who launched British *Cosmo*!

The magazine could hardly fail to make a huge impact. After the double dose of exposure in the colour magazine, the actual launch was like an offensive. A total of £1,000,000 was assigned for publicity, with national television promotion and no shortage of free advertising space in *The Times* and the *Sunday Times*. Six-sheet posters went up on the hoardings from 1 October to herald the arrival of the new title. The magazine was perfect-bound and priced at only £1, very competitive with the existing glossies. The first six issues claimed an average circulation of 230,000 and the early NRS readership figures showed an up-market profile of seventy-one per cent ABC1 with sixty-seven per cent under the age of thirty-five, statistics that outshone the rival *Vogue*. *Vogue*, however, still held the trump card of being the trade's arbiter of fashion, not an easy commercial mountain for *Elle* to climb. But the first issue was thick with advertising, full of confidence and very lively. It was, and is, an efficient, readable fashion magazine which appeals to the younger reader. Murdoch sold his fifty per cent stake in the magazine to Hachette in 1988 and EMAP bought the half stake in 1992, taking responsibility for the running of the title. The circulation still hovers around 220,000, which presents it with attractive advertising potential under the EMAP umbrella.

The 1980s were still bursting with launches, making it the most active decade in the history of women's magazines in the sheer number of new launches, several of which were to change the publishing scene. Minor events included the frustrated launch of *Tomorrow* from the fashion designer Katherine Hamnett. Her aspiration to be a leading publishing player was articulated strongly:

> I want to synthesize the things which seem important to me from fashion, art, music and news to tough investigative journalism and get them under cover. And I want to shock – there are things happening in the world just now which threaten us all, as well as providing top-level entertainment. I want to use my magazine to shout my mouth off about them.

The magazine was planned to sell in her shops as well as the newstrade, but eight hours before the first issue went to press she pulled out – a classic case of publisher interruptus. In the end, one issue did appear before *Tomorrow* became yesterday.

Other titles included *Knit & Stitch*, *Lipstick* (for models *manquées*) and the German *Sandra*, for needlewomen. Another knitting journal, *Caroline*, contributed to global publishing by launching simultaneously in Belgium, Luxemburg, France, Germany, Austria and Switzerland, as well as the UK, with a total print run of 800,000, of which ten per cent was bestowed on this country. CFE Publishing launched *Traditional Homes*, a £1 monthly for the owners of older properties; there are six million pre-1919 homes in this country. A curiosity from Birmingham was *Frills*, 'the feminine magazine'. The editor glibly welcomed her readers: 'Hello and welcome to *Frills* – the first magazine specifically created for today's fashion-conscious, feminine woman. The magazine you've been waiting for and the magazine we believe every woman needs.' The editorial, unfortunately, was an amateurish mishmash and the company swiftly went into liquidation, owing thousands of pounds. *Lean Living* aimed at the three million known vegetarians in this country, 'or those with meat-free eating habits'. The first issue carried a tempting cover mount of a lemon fruit-and-nut bar. Also came *Veg*, a glossy monthly 'not just for vegetarians' which took an obsessive interest in vegetables.

Redwood Publishing, the specialists in contract publishing, were retained by Marks & Spencer to produce their new magazine. Aimed at M & S card holders, it sells in three hundred stores and achieves a sale of one million copies. This is a sure-fire formula with the editorial and the advertising content closely monitored by the store.

In 1985, while I was Publishing Director of *Good Housekeeping*, it occurred to me that there was a distinct possibility that the Hearst title *Country Living* could be successful over here – as a concept, not an editorial style. *Country Living* had scored a remarkable success in the States, finding an immediate response not only to its depiction of rural life but also to the return to traditional values. We decided to test the market here by putting the toe of a green welly into the publishing water. Because of the prestige of *Good Housekeeping*, we billed our first issue as *Good Housekeeping*'s *Country Living*. The success was instantaneous, with a complete sell-out for both the May and September pilot issues. The ambience of a country magazine was obviously a winner and the decision was made to publish bi-monthly in 1986. Carlton Publishing seemed to be impressed by our successful idea and announced *Country Homes & Interiors*, to be published monthly from the spring. That spurred us to go straight to monthly frequency, which we did from March 1986. *Country Homes*, as the title implies, has concentrated on the domestic country life, whereas *Country Living* takes a much broader view of rural matters, achieving a remarkable circulation of over 180,000 copies and backed by the successful *Country Living* Fair held in London each spring. An impressive 750,000 women read *Country Living* and half a million read *Country Homes*.

Two feminist magazines introduced themselves in 1985. *Women's Review* was launched as a co-operative woman's title. 'The magazine', said the editor, is born out of a desire to create a free space where the voices of many women can be heard.... The main aim of the *Women's Review* co-operative is not to write the entire magazine, setting up yet another closed circuit of ideas, but to open a magazine up to include the expression of divergent beliefs and styles.

Everywoman billed itself as 'the only current affairs magazine for Britain and Ireland which is written for women by women'. It claimed to bridge the gap between the glossies like *Cosmopolitan* and the committed feminism of *Spare Rib*. Neither of the new titles carried colour or more than token political and feminist advertising. *Everywoman* carried a regular sports page for women in sport.

Cachet appeared in the autumn of 1985 aimed at the four million women sized sixteen and over. The editor made out her case:

Full-bodied is a popular adjective used to describe good wine and conjures up the anticipation and absolute enjoyment of a rich, smooth subtle taste to excite the palate. If only the very same adjective, when applied to the human female form, conjured up the same excitement! *Cachet* intends to demonstrate firmly how making anyone over a size sixteen glamorous is definitely NOT an impossibility.... All our fashion will be worn and photographed on gorgeous large models, no smaller than size eighteen.

A year later came *Extra Special* ('Beauty Comes in all Sizes').

Half the women in Britain need a sixteen or larger dress size. Yet in a society that worships the ultra-slim, in which natural curves are called bulges and to weigh more than nine stone is to risk a 'Fatty' label, the larger woman has been made to feel inferior.

There was definitely a market. But *Cachet* only published one issue, suffering from under-financing. It resurfaced a year later, publishing three issues. *Extra Special* had similar financial problems but, surprisingly, Robert Maxwell bought it in 1988. He declared it would go monthly with a print order of 175,000 – and then promptly closed it. So both titles had short and unhappy lives, despite the real possibilities of the market. No major publisher has since taken up the cudgels despite the obvious potential, though in 1993 *Pretty Big* emerged as a quarterly.

The publishers of *TV Times* (then Independent Television Publications before they sold out to IPC) were eager to extend their publishing franchise into women's magazines. They had experienced a flop earlier in the 1980s with a quarterly called *First Lady* which survived for only one issue. Now they went full tilt for the popular end of the market by producing *Chat*, a tabloid newspaper masquerading as a magazine. (Nowadays we have magazines masquerading as tabloid newspapers.) *Chat* was unashamedly down-market, with the low cover price of eighteen pence and a print-run of one million copies. Half the thirty-two pages were in colour but the printing was the low quality of newsprint. The editor, Lori Miles, was seduced from IPC's *Mizz*, and she set the tone: 'We're really a cross between a newspaper and a magazine. Every Tuesday we'll be giving you the news that affects women and families, new ideas, money-saving tips and your favourite celebrities... in fact, everything and anything that women today *Chat* about.' The concept was put together with the assistance of the German company Axel Springer, and based on the style of their own magazine *Bild den Frau*. ITP said the magazine would appeal to the busy woman and would give her a great deal of advice and information in an easy-to-read format. The advertising policy was clearly defined by Lori Miles: 'We don't want posey ads, it won't be pretentious.'

The project was severely criticized by the media business as being a down-market mess. This was harsh judgement, since the aim must have been to create a weekly newspaper for women on the same intellectual level as readers of the *Sun*. The circulation settled down at about 500,000. After IPC's acquisition, *Chat* moved into conventional magazine format and still sells around the same figure.

D.C. Thomson, ever watchful of market trends, decided that they too could go down-market and produced *Celebrity*, 'the sparkling new weekly'. This was printed gravure with a cover price of thirty pence and a more modest initial print run of 500,000. *Celebrity* was full of jokes, celebrity profiles (Steve Davis, Felicity Kendall, Princess Di) cartoons, problem letters and funny picture stories. The circulation soon matched the editorial status and sank to under 130,000. Within two years D.C. Thomson killed it off, shifting it into their *Weekly News*.

The year 1986 saw the *Blitzkreig* hit British publishing. Up to now all the competition in the industry had been indigenous, except for the vicarious products of American publishers: magazines like *Vogue*, *Good Housekeeping*, *House & Garden* and *Cosmopolitan*. These were published, and considerably if not totally Anglicized, by satellite British companies of their American parents. But on to the British publishing stage came the Demon King. The Germans had arrived. The eagle had landed.

The first missile to be lobbed, with all the thunder and surprise of a V2 rocket, was *Prima*. Grühner & Jahr, the mighty German publishing company, was looking for global expansion; in Germany, *Prima* was already selling 700,000 in a massively overcrowded and saturated market. It had already been launched in France, reaching a breath-taking 1,400,000 sale in rapid time. The Germans felt the British market was waiting for them. Their target audience was clear: women between the ages of twenty-five to fifty-four, and the product was classless and practical, representing good value for money. Lots of recipes, homecrafts, beauty and health, knitting and sewing, gardening, pets, childcare, do-it-yourself, travel and high street fashions. The whole shebang was a glorious return to the old standards, the *hausfrau* syndrome of good wives and good mothers. Nothing could have been further from the sexcess of the 1970s: we were back to the basics of happy family life. At seventy-five pence a copy *Prima* was superb value, even without the brilliant marketing stroke that shook the home-grown publishers: every issue of *Prima* contained a printed paper pattern, considered to be worth a pound on its own merits. Another *coup* was the capture of Iris Burton, the editor of *Woman's Own*, to run the magazine.

Prima was launched on an advertising budget of £1.5 million, with the ubiquitous television campaign emphasizing the practical, crafts element of the magazine. And, of course, the paper pattern. *Prima* would not be concerned with soap stars, the royals, gossip or horoscopes, but rather the home and the family. As well as the heavy television advertising there was substantial use of commercial radio, the middle-brow tabloids and 2,500 poster sites throughout the country. This was no home counties magazine – it was a national launch for all socioeconomic groups. The first issue sold out of the 400,000 print run and the second issue sold out of the increased print run of 650,000.

The Germans' declared intention was to achieve a substantial circulation success. Advertising volume was secondary to this ambition – get the circulation and the advertisers would flock to the magazine. The publisher stated that the German High Command were content to wait seven years before seeing a return on their investment. The priority was to establish a publishing bridgehead in this country. And success followed success, with *Prima* achieving the magic million circulation the following year. No other monthly consumer magazine sold on the bookstalls had ever reached that dizzy and exhilarating height.

What was the secret of *Prima's* extraordinary success in a saturated market? Certainly the explosive and efficient launch campaign. Definitely the sales gimmick of the paper pattern (later quietly eliminated). But probably the leading factor was the timing. Women welcomed this return to the simpler traditional features. The challenges were familiar and fun. Housewives could hold their heads up again without having them shot at by the trendies, the feminists and the sexologists. *Prima* created the support to get on with life and to look after the family, the cocker spaniel and the rockery, and one million *Prima* buyers will attest to it!

But if *Prima* was the advance guard, the 1987 arrival of the main army from Germany was devastating to the shell-shocked British magazine bosses. *Best* came bursting out of the blue like a great bomb, again from Grühner & Jahr. There had been ugly rumours of a German weekly, and doubtless IPC were putting up the barbed wire and filling the stirrup-pumps. But the explosion, when it came, was a total surprise. The chosen month was August, definitely not a month during which any British publisher would choose to launch. It's a month when business is quiet and all the readers of the women's weeklies are toasting themselves on the beaches of the Costa Brava. Not only did the Germans choose the month of August, but they pinpointed 12 August, the very day that sporting men are out on the grouse moor potting at birds. *Best* was edited by Iris Burton, and modelled on *Femme Actuelle*, Grühner & Jahr's French title. Very little advertising had been sold for the new magazine for the simple reason that the launch had been precipitate and secret. There had just not been enough time to hawk the project around the agencies and the advertisers.

As Grühner & Jahr said at the time of the shock launch:

> One of the critical things about *Best* is the destiny. Our research
> showed that there is a measure of discontent with the weeklies
> and a feeling that they don't go far enough. Fun and
> entertainment are very important, but at the same time people
> want to be treated as grown-ups.

The actual notice given to the newstrade and the advertising business was a breath-taking two weeks. The traditional gestation period for a major magazine had always been a recognized six months with a bit of fanfare. But this was panzer publishing, taking the enemy completely by surprise by the sheer weight of armour and rapidity of movement.

Best cost thirty-five pence. It was devoid of the staple IPC diet of royalty, Coronation Street and gossipy features. It was full of short, sharp newsy stories, but in good fun. The lighter elements were backed by plenty of sound advice on money, consumer affairs, legal rights, health, careers and cookery. There were competitions galore and profiles of the famous. *Best* was informative and 'a good read'. Crafts were left to *Prima*; *Best* was intended to be a light read over a cup of coffee with plenty of relevant, helpful information, tersely presented. It was soon selling over one million copies, a figure that would be halved over the next six years.

There was, among the weekly magazine publishers, a xenophobic alarm at this parvenu magazine with a simple formula, which could sweep into the market and take a million copies off the bookstalls. The advertising weekly magazine *Campaign* commented that '*Best* was shaking up the meat and two veg approach in favour of a "Nouvelle" magazine one'. Very indigestible. But worse (or *wurst*) was to come.

Bauer, Germany's biggest magazine publisher, could not permit their rivals to steal a march on them. With the same element of surprise, they rushed out another weekly called *Bella*. Competitively priced at only twenty-nine pence, it aimed smack at the traditional IPC weeklies. The slogan 'Something for Everyone Every Week' meant a formula that was far from novel. In fact, it strictly followed the old safe route of letters, health, gardening, knitting patterns and a knock at the Royal Family: 'Do you think our royals are royal enough? Write in and let us know. Next week: The taming of Princess Pushy', horoscopes, shopping, sex problems, cooking, childcare, a bit of Joan Collins, money matters, fiction, Family Doctor, etc. The latter had a smattering of Dr Delvin about it: 'Whenever I get an erection it is distinctly kinked. My wife has started calling me Concorde....'

This was not Bauer's first incursion into foreign markets. Like Grühner & Jahr, they found the only way to expand out of their crowded home market was to publish overseas. They had launched *Woman's World* in the USA but had taken five years to achieve a circulation of 1.4 million. *Bella* was a British version of *Woman's World* and bore a family likeness to another of their German titles, *Tina*. The name *Bella* (as the name *Woman's World* was *verboten* here) was chosen for the UK, according to a Bauer spokesman, Mr Weidenholtz, because they 'wanted to get away from the plethora of titles in the UK called *Woman's This* and *Woman's That*, which all sounded the same. *Bella* was chosen as an all-purpose name with international credibility. It may be thought of as Italian but that doesn't bother me because the connotation is not negative'.

Bella's sales were slow to start, even with a lot of fancy sampling techniques. The previous week's issue would be mailed out with a stapled wrapper bearing the statement: '*Bella*. This is your free copy of last week's issue. Pick up this week's from your local newsagent now!'

The sales of *Bella* have always been reported as being over the one million level but Bauer has never joined the Audit Bureau of Circulation and issued audited statements. Subsequently Bauer has launched *Take a Break* (1990) and *TV Quick* (1991). *Take a Break* enjoys the top sale of all women's weeklies with a circulation of 1.4 million.

The battered Brits, still reeling from this burst of Teutonic activity, marketing innovation and money pumped into their markets, were to be confronted with yet more foreign shocks. From America came *W*, a British version of the famous Fairchild New York fashion bible – the arbiter of Fifth and Seventh Avenues. The British franchise was bought by an ebullient Irishman, Kevin Kelly, who had launched *The World of Interiors* and sold it on to Condé Nast. But *W* was peculiarly shaped and packaged. The pages, in newspaper format, were nineteen-inches long, and the whole magazine, which consisted of seven sections, was packaged in a plastic wrapper. The editor was Jane Proctor, who went on to edit *Tatler* after *W*'s failure. Her leading editorial chortled:

> Welcome to the launch issue of *W*, Britain's first fortnightly fashion newspaper. *W* is the British edition of the wonderful American *W*, a relationship we are extremely proud of.... *W* is unique in more ways than one. It's a newspaper and has the advantages of immediacy, punch and speed. But at the same time it has all the benefits of a glossy magazine with its superb reproduction and paper.... Add our Eye pages, snappy reportage, stunning portraits of people and their homes and the cream of the international collections, and you have *W* – a mix that is colourful, clever and classy.

The subscription card tucked into the first issue was no less diffident: 'Worldly, Wicked and Wonderful.... Pure self-indulgence. For those who want to know who's who, who's wearing who, who's doing what to who, and who cares!'

W's initial print-run was 60,000, with an estimated settle-down forecast of 40,000. But the magazine was to run for less than a year, launching in November 1987 and going belly-up in October 1988. Maybe it could never capture the in-crowd, cognisant camaraderie of the mix of society and the rag trade which is the secret of the New York original. Over here, the fashion trade has its press and society is well catered for by the glossies. *Vogue* crosses the divide of trade and customer so satisfactorily that perhaps *W* was simply looked upon as superfluous. The bookstall sales must have suffered from the plastic wrapping. Trussed up like a Soho sex manual, *W* was impossible for potential buyers to pick up and browse through. The publisher's hope must have lain with subscriptions becoming a must for everybody in fashion – but that hope was never fulfilled.

New Woman, another American import, came over from the newly established Murdoch Magazines. *New Woman* had started in the States as a *Cosmopolitan* look-alike but had been underfunded before being purchased by Murdoch as part of his global magazine empire. The editor of the new British version, Frankie McGowan, explicitly defined the magazine's eponymous reader in its first issue:

> A new woman is fun to be with, not a formidable challenge –
> someone who is softer, more feminine than the myth of superwoman.
> We have come a long way since we were force-fed the illusion of
> that finger-snapping, high-flying executive in her power suit pushing
> her way up the executive ladder while running the ideal home, perfect
> children and lover, fitting in aerobics classes on the side. No longer
> are we afraid to say that she was a figment of the media's
> imagination and nothing to do with the real us – women married or
> single, who are daily balancing home, husband or lover, children,
> friends and jobs. Realistic enough to know that we can't have it all,
> but optimistic enough to give it our best shot.... From the intimate
> to the frivolous, from the realistic to the idealistic, we are talking not
> about you, but to you. Welcome to your own magazine, New
> Woman, every one of you!'

The early *New Woman* was light years away from the later (EMAP) version in the 1990s. The first issue now seems almost staid with a strong emphasis on relationships: lack of self-confidence, how to get on with his kids, successful step-parenting, unrequited love, competing couples, how to stress-proof your life, child maintenance. These were some of the problems set before the reader in issue number one. Getting over the sack seemed a more important topic than getting into the sack, surely a preoccupation of today's magazine. Straightforward, sober, sisterly advice was the order of the day with none of the overt features on sex, so much part of the passionate young women's titles these days. The serious subjects are still covered, campaigns waged and plenty of advice given – but *New Woman* has joined the ranks of the magazines that like to spell it all out, a leader in the contemporary vogue for forthright, frank and explicit sex advice and instruction – without a hint of titillation, of course. On the other side of the coin, it is only fair to say that *New Woman* runs serious issues and some of its campaigns have won awards in the publishing industry.

And then came the Spanish Armada. *¡Hola!* is one of Spain's most successful weekly magazines, a sort of *El Picture Post* full of gossipy photo journalism about international celebrities. The magazine is owned by a private family company and they saw the potential of a British version directed at a nation of snobs, voyeurs, celebrity hunters and royalty worshippers. The new magazine was named *Hello!*, which is about as near to *¡Hola!* as you can get. The publishing arrangements were unique, with two editors, one in Madrid and one in London. The British editor, Maggie Goodman, moved over from *Company*, and Madrid was run by Maggie Koumi, erstwhile editor of *19*. The magazine is printed in Spain and shipped over to the UK, with dramatically short editorial dead-lines and the capacity to run whole photo-stories within hours to catch the weekly shipments. The first issue appeared in May 1988, the begin-ning of a phenomenal success story which, once again, would amaze and confound British publishers and pundits. The new British readers were kept ignorant of the Spanish origins of the new magazine and Maggie Goodman was careful to avoid any breath of Iberian involvement in her cheerful upbeat editorial:

If I have to sum up the tone of the magazine in three words, I can do it easily. *Hello!* is different!... First impressions must be of colour, brilliant colour, and lots of it. We've all been educated over the last decades to appreciate the impact of colour, on television and in the cinema, so why shouldn't we expect the same standards when we turn to a magazine? Every picture tells a story and in *Hello!* we make sure we give enough space to cover the story and in depth. Because of our short deadlines we can get the news to you quickly. So if you want exclusivity and if you want an inside look at royal tours, important events of the week, the happenings in the lives of the famous, adventures and amazing feats – and always the most surprising news – from now on you'll know where to find it....
Hello! is a magazine for women which we hope will appeal to the

whole family. Far from dealing exclusively with 'women's subjects' we cover a wide spectrum and there should be plenty to interest everyone with a sense of curiosity....

And 'in depth' is what you got. The first issue covered the wedding of Burt Reynolds. There were eighteen pictures of Burt, up the aisle, signing the registry, lighting a candle, showing the ring, cutting the cake, wiping tears from his eyes, kissing his bride, kissing his mother, kissing his horse, off to the reception by coach and off on the honeymoon by helicopter. Plus sundry pictures of the bride, the bridesmaids, mother, mother-in-law, father-in-law, etc. The Queen only got ten pictures, but she was the second feature. Ivana Trump only got seven.

But mock ye not. The over-the-top voyeurism of the rich, famous and infamous captured an immediate and passionately devoted readership in this country. *Hello!* is a feast for the curious and the prying, a banquet for armchair peeping-toms. *Hello!* draws on the world of the stars, whether film, theatre, royal, television or society. Doors have been opened to the cameras of *Hello!* – positively flung open – so that the rich and famous (even if sometimes slipping) can show themselves in the best possible light. The gossip, the snooping, the privacy invasion is utterly benign. No smear, no innuendo, no mockery ever appears in *Hello!* And that is why the doors are flung open: here is the perfect PR vehicle for displaying to the public what a beautiful house you live in, what exquisite taste you have and what a really lovely person you are. Other magazines may be intrusive or derogatory but *Hello!* is the Mr Nice Guy of the gossip media.

And what a success *Hello!* has seen. The weekly sales simply soared, reaching a staggering 470,000 copies by 1993. The pundits were reeling, the opposition gob-smacked. The newstrade found it difficult to believe that a 75p weekly (the launch price) could possibly succeed on the bookstalls. *Hello!* has not only succeeded but it has sailed past every expectation of the publishers. It has since added television listings and lost Maggie Goodman as editor, but it still stands high and profitable. *Hello!* must be marked as one of the most successful women's magazines launched since the war.

The last invader of the 1980s came from France in the shape of a British version of *Marie Claire*. The French publisher had originally intended a cooperative deal with the *Daily Mail* Group but this fell through and a marriage with IPC was hastily arranged. This was fortuitous for

IPC, as *Marie Claire* has turned out to be one of the big magazine successes of all time. The betrothal of France and Britain was not entirely straightforward as there was already a fiancée in the shape of *Fashion Folio*, née *Folio*. This was an IPC one-shot, a tentative big toe in the choppy waters of fashion publishing. IPC, aiming at ABC1 women, described *Folio* as 'an understandable format explaining the season's looks and how to achieve them'. The one-shot sold well and a second issue was produced with the further announcement that *Fashion Folio* would become a monthly in the spring of 1988. But events moved quickly when the French came a-wooing, and *Fashion Folio* was abandoned in favour of the joint venture *Marie Claire*, with Glenda Bailey as editor.

The very first issue of *Marie Claire* smelled of success. Two hundred-and-fifty-two pages of fashion and beauty, with all the customary magazine departments, but strongly laced with serious features. That first issue took a look at Arabia behind the veil, carried a profile on Audrey Hepburn, a feature on rape and rapists, a story on Northern Ireland's Catholic women and an investigation into cellulite – all robust stuff, making an intelligent package of readable material. Perhaps *Marie Claire* usurped the position *Nova* might have occupied if it had not been so smart-arse in its later days. And there was no secrecy or shyness about the Gallic origins – rather impossible with that title!

Glenda Bailey led with her chin: 'Welcome to the first UK edition of *Marie Claire*; a magazine that originated in France and is already an international success in four other countries, thanks to a unique approach which combines breadth of content with stylish treatment.' Say no more. That sentence sums up the success of *Marie Claire*: a source of incisive and serious editorial features wrapped in a comfortable layer of fashion and beauty. Bailey continued:

Each month stimulating and thought-provoking articles will encompass countries, cultures and issues world-wide. We will interview stars who have more to offer than mere glamour; emotional matters will be treated constructively yet with compassion. We aim to produce articles which will be not just talked about today but which will be the big news of tomorrow....

Five years later the magazine staggered with weight – not only the sheer poundage of some of its issues, which reach three hundred pages, but also the weight of the awards they have picked up. In *Marie Claire*'s short life it has won ten major publishing awards: thrice magazine of the year, twice editor of the year and sundry others for features and campaigns. If there was an award for the most awards, it would go to *Marie Claire*. With circulation bounding up over the magic 350,000 the magazine was a godsend to IPC when the *Daily Mail* deal went sour, and the editorial formula has remained consistently successful.

And while the continental incursions into the soft underbelly of the British market were going on, the Brits (i.e., IPC) were busy in their bunker. There can be little doubt that the launch and incredible success of *Prima* had been a custard pie in the face of IPC. The follow up of *Best* and *Bella* were equally morale-shattering. British pride was at stake – and more to the point, British profits. The solution to the *Prima* problem was obvious, if expensive. Bring out your own *Prima*, copy the technique, imitate the action of the tiger. So in February 1988, *Essentials* emerged, backed by the biggest launch in IPC's history, with a publicity budget of £2.5 million. The first three issues were supported by a budget of £1 million on television alone. The theme of the new monthly was 'practical' – a direct howitzer attack on *Prima*'s rediscovered niche. The cover price was seventy-five pence, the initial print run 700,000 and the advertiser guaranteed sales of 500,000.

The *Essentials* gimmicks were also a direct onslaught. There were fifty-six file pages, ready-punched and perforated, which could be put away in a three-ringed binder (worth £1.75) given away with the first issue. There were index cards for cooking, knitting, sewing, money matters, health, beauty, etc. And – something only the Germans had thought of before – each issue would contain a paper pattern! The invader had been given a taste of his own medicine, and a spit right in the eye. As the editor, Liz Glaze, said:

> *Essentials* is the first magazine designed for you to enjoy, use...
> and keep. It's a simple idea – but such a good one, we're amazed no
> one's thought of it before! As well as all the best ingredients of a
> great magazine – fun reads and serious features, high street fashion
> and home-making, interviews with people in the news – *Essentials*
> gives you fifty-six special pull-out pages and, with our first issue, a
> beautiful binder to keep them in. Month by month this will grow into
> your own invaluable reference file.

Essentials did well, with good sales in the 750,000 range. Although sales are now down to under 400,000, the counter-attack was a palpable hit, so much so that IPC, with their dander up and their juices flowing, turned the tables on the continentals by taking the magazine to France and other countries in a series of joint deals with foreign publishers. The invasion, and the counter-attack, proved one point beyond doubt: despite the vogue for orgasms, sexual athletics and extremely candid concentrations on things below the belt, there was definitely still an audience for home-making, crafts and traditional values.

But from this welcome sign of IPC's retaliation in producing one of their best successes since their conglomeration, we now turn to look at one of their biggest failures.

Eight
1989–1994

The launch of *Riva* was probably the most expensive failure in the volatile history of women's magazines, and certainly the swiftest loss of a very large investment in the medium.

Carlton Magazines, still a separate IPC satellite in 1988, announced the launch of a new weekly, *Riva*. It was billed as a 'super launch', with an investment of £3.5 million and an ambition to sell 350,000 weekly copies. The editor, Sally O'Sullivan, moved over from Carlton's *Options* to launch the new title. The Carlton publicity machine thundered out:

> It will be different from anything else on the market. We will be aiming to pick up readers from the existing weeklies but we also plan on attracting readers from the glossy monthlies, so it is hard to say who our competition will be. *Riva* will contain the style and quality of a monthly with the pace and immediacy of a weekly.

The cover price was set at fifty pence and the first cover was a clever half-gatefold. In the first issue, Sally O'Sullivan explained:

> In case you were wondering, yes there is room for another new woman's magazine. Because while others tell you they're different, this time you can see for yourself. *Riva* is a weekly unlike other weeklies. It's glossy and stylish, just like the expensive monthly magazines, yet it's pacey, instant and newsy. Most magazines take weeks to produce. *Riva* takes days....

Most magazines take years to flop – *Riva* took weeks.

The build-up to the launch was impressive. Sixteen-sheet posters appeared everywhere. Carlton announced that the first issue was to be increased from eighty to one hundred-and-four pages to cope with 'the high demand'. Heady with anticipated success, Carlton closed their magazine *Look Now* to concentrate their resources on *Riva*. The initial print run of the first issue, dated 13 September was 590,000. The issue sold 350,000 copies. Within two weeks, Reed International, the owners of IPC and Carlton, announced that Carlton would be merged into IPC. In another fortnight the gimmick of the cover gatefold was abandoned to cut production costs. IPC admitted that Carlton's circulation estimates had been too optimistic and set new targets of 300,000 weekly. But by 12 October, issue number six sold only 160,000 copies and IPC slashed the advertising rates. And on 18 October it was black hats all round, as Carlton announced the closure of the magazine.

The post-mortems began. The final loss of the magazine was estimated to have been £3 million. Colin Reeves-Smith of IPC blamed the misjudgement over launch costs. 'The cost of promoting the title was greatly underestimated. The total investment needed in order to get the magazine accepted by the target audience would have been much, much greater than the £7 million originally set aside,' he told *Magazine Week*. He pointed also to 'the reluctance on the part of British women to accept a new magazine formula'. Tens of thousands of pounds had to be returned to advertisers each week as rebates were called in. Agencies felt that the title failed to live up to its pre-launch hype and that the formula of a monthly posing as a weekly was too *outré* for the British public.

When the smoke had cleared away, IPC was £3 million down the pan, seventy staff were made redundant, *Look Now* had been the patsy and Sally O'Sullivan went on holiday to consider her future with the company. Somebody at IPC must have said 'Oops!'

Was the magazine that bad? Certainly not. A retrospective view of the seven issues shows a smart, literate, amusing, well laid-out, well-photographed magazine with gossipy pages about the rich and famous. There were good pieces of reportage and even a touch of *Hello!* in some of the personality pictures. But it was a weekly with a monthly trying to get out. Launched as a monthly, with less hype and less horrendous up-front costs, *Riva* might still be with us today.

Meanwhile, things were rumbling along in the previously neglected homes front of publishing. Traditional features were middle- and upper-class residences with pretty interiors and beautiful gardens. *House & Garden, Homes & Gardens, World of Interiors, Ideal Home* and *Country Homes & Interiors* represented the affluent world of people who could live in and enjoy superior property. The big publishers were restless: were they missing out on a market of millions of home-owners who lived not in old rectories, converted oast houses or stockbroker Tudor, but in semis or even flats – and were equally house-proud? Both National Magazines and IPC announced one-shot specials in 1988. *Good Housekeeping* produced a banded issue on *Good Housekeeping* called *GH Homes* and IPC declared that they would be producing a bookstall one-off called *Beautiful Living*. In the event, National Magazines got out of the starting gate first by publishing *House Beautiful* three times a year in 1989. The IPC proposal never appeared.

House Beautiful was bursting with innovation, following up the fashionable binder concept with a Homefax file, which they sold to readers. Each issue contains six Homefax tear-out cards, which slot into the binders to make a collection of subjects from wiring a three-pin plug to changing a tap washer. *House Beautiful* is crammed with domestic features all beamed to the more modest suburban home. It also contains one unique crowd-pulling idea: pages called 'On the House', containing dozens of give-away items such as cushions, candles, catalogues, stencils, packets of seeds, paint brushes – free to the first two hundred or sometimes five hundred readers who fill in the coupons. *House Beautiful*'s timing was spot on, and found an immediate audience of home-owners eager to improve their homes. Many were unable to trade up because of mortgage problems and the static state of the housing market, so they were avidly seeking ideas and inspirations. And *House Beautiful* is stuffed with ideas – indeed that word always appears on the front cover, along with the titillation of making the best of small spaces, clever kitchens, instant gardens, brighter bathrooms, mortgage problems and solutions and home improvements generally. This was *House & Gardens* for the masses and *House Beautiful* was rewarded with instant success and a circulation growing to well over 300,000 in four years of publishing, quickly establishing itself as the top-selling homes monthly, much to the chagrin of *Ideal Home*, the former contender.

Such a brilliant concept could not long be unchallenged in the dog-eat-dog world of magazines. Two imitators were soon to appear, *Home Flair* and *Perfect Home*. IPC threw themselves into the battle in 1993 with a complete *doppelgänger* called *Homes & Ideas* bearing a startling likeness to the original.

In the spring of 1988 Focus Magazines, in a joint venture with the BBC, produced the *Clothes Show Magazine*, one of the early overt link-ups by the BBC with publishing. The Clothes Show itself enjoyed an audience of eight million and the magazine, according to the editor, would pick up where the programme left off. But the magazine had a flaccid 'trade' look about it rather than the bounce and verve expected and associated with the programme. The venture was taken over by Redwood, who had a close association with the BBC until the corporation decided to run their own publishing, and the magazine went on to sell 170,000 copies. Although the gratuitous on-air publicity was halted for BBC magazines the publisher is still able to publicize the title to advertisers as 'no other magazine can offer 661,000 solus readers and tap the ready-made market produced by the Clothes Show programme and Clothes Show Live. This combination of magazine, plus TV, plus exhibition generates its own powerful brand'.

Monolithic publishing corporations can get bigger in two ways. They can be creative and innovative by inventing new titles, finding novel markets or stimulating old ones. This is an expensive route to take which can be richly rewarded with success or uncomfortably expensive when they see their offspring falter and expire, as evidenced by the examples in this history. The other way forward for the mega rich corporations is to buy out the opposition and go on a shopping spree, picking off the competition and sweeping their titles into your basket. IPC certainly did this when, as part of the cash-rich Reed International, they purchased *Family Circle* and *Living* from Thomson International in 1988, and then *TV Times* and *Chat* from Independent Television Publications in 1989. The first acquisition was known to have cost £28 million and the latter a rumoured £200 million.

The sale of the supermarket titles was engineered by Thomson. No longer a media empire since selling *The Times* to Rupert Murdoch and their television franchise in Scotland, Thomson was obsessed with its considerable oil interests. A short look into the future convinced them that their exclusive deal with the supermarkets was under threat; the superstores had discovered magazines as a useful source of revenue and profit. Tesco was already selling two hundred titles and other titles were making incursions into the check-out racks once held sacred by Thomson. IPC bought out Thomson in a blind auction and in no time the whole picture was altered: the check-outs were full of IPC magazines and *Family Circle* and *Living* began to appear in the newsagents.

Murdoch also wanted to get out of magazines. His launch of *Mirabella* in October 1990 was a short-lived and expensive flop. The magazine was a clone of the American magazine but as its launch coincided with Murdoch's international financial pressures there was little time or will to persevere with the glossy title. At £2.20 an issue the magazine seemed aimless. Even the editor Lesley White tried to answer the criticism that

> *Mirabella* was just another glossy indulgence. If [the critics] were
> expecting to be answered with a list of statistics, a newstrade
> analysis and a neatly defined gap in the market theory, they went
> away disappointed. For although two hundred quality pages are born
> of a commercial venture, they are also, above all else, an over-riding,
> fingers-crossed act of faith.

Maybe more than fingers should have been crossed as *Mirabella* was to survive for only nine issues with trade estimates of sales between 30,000 and 60,000. Murdoch sold his magazine company to the ever-eager EMAP who were keen to acquire the potential of *New Woman* for their burgeoning women's group. Students of these peregrinations may recall that Murdoch had sold half his stake in *Elle* to Hachette and EMAP were soon to swoop to take control of the title from the French. The voracious EMAP also took over six titles from Argus Press, adding *Slimming*, *Parents*, *Mother & Baby*, *Mother*, *Here's Health* and *Successful Slimming* to their portfolio. In a few months they closed *Mother* (née 1936) and *Successful Slimming*. In 1991 they bought *Traditional Homes* from Burleigh and *Select* and *Kerang* from United Consumer Magazines.

The last big launch of the 1980s was IPC's *Me*, a 40p weekly backed by £50,000 of research, £1 million on development and a hefty launch publicity budget. *Me* was IPC's face-to-face with the German *Bella* and *Best*. IPC explained the launch as their entry into the younger end of the weekly market. Liz Glaze, the editor, said that she had been travelling the country asking women what they wanted from a new weekly. The answers were clear: 'Fashions we can afford.' 'Beauty ideas that won't make us look silly.' 'A good laugh.' 'Features about real people.' 'News about things we can buy in our own high street or by mail order.' Plus, of course, recipes, patterns, practical advice, gossip. If we seem to recognize the editorial formula as coming with us down the years, another ingredient was added: a pull-out ring binder section on cooking, sewing, knitting and the home. We could learn how to change a plug or repair a fuse again. And... a paper pattern! So *Me* was to drive a readership wedge between the German weeklies and the practical monthly *Prima*. The circulation of *Me* fell to a low of 358,000 in the latter part of 1993, making it IPC's lowest-selling weekly.

Where there's life, there's death, and IPC, faced 'with tough advertising conditions', closed *Woman's World* in May 1990. Closure or sale rumours had been firmly denied the year before, after the magazine had a sales slump and a disastrous truncating of the title to *WW* – the old formula for possible regeneration which always precedes death. The new slogan 'It's Big, it's Beautiful and it's Full of Surprises' must have rung hollow to the staff at the sudden demise. Lack of advertising and a falling circulation were certainly to blame, but the real bugbear was a lack of branding and identity: it became just another mid-market title.

With the successfull launch of *House Beautiful*, the market for homes magazines began to move. *Period Living* came from EMAP Elan, a title directed at people living in older homes 'who enjoy the sense of history, the elegance, the atmosphere, the character, but can also brave the dry rot, the damp, the seemingly inexhaustible demand on the pocket and patience, to see that character lovingly restored'. Argus had the same idea with *Renovate*. But the intended big launch in the field was *Metropolitan Home*, a joint venture between the American publisher Meredith, who owned the title in the States, and Harmsworth, part of the *Daily Mail* group. This was a big, expensive venture into architecture, decoration and furnishings. The British editorial team 'will have a fresh, journalistic approach to what has traditionally been decorating or nostalgia-led home interest coverage. Our reports will cover what's new, what's good and what's amusing in the areas of design, food, restaurants, transport, gardening, architecture, interiors, travel. In other words, the trends, events and people that influence the way we live'. The words of the editor Dee Nolan. But *Metropolitan Home* lacked advertising support and closed with a disappointing sale of 40,000 after going bi-monthly as a life-saving measure.

One of the puzzling post-war phenomena in magazine sales has been the sustained success of puzzle magazines, originally a popular continental pastime. There are as many as fifty magazines on the market which live on their cover price alone, carrying little or no advertising. In 1990 the German publisher Bauer decided to take the puzzle formula and mix it with the well-tried women's weekly feature magazine. Out came *Take a Break*, with the early issues reduced from 35p to 10p. *Take a Break*'s *métier* is the puzzles and competitions; twenty pages of puzzles with £25,000 worth of prizes in every issue. In the first issue you could win a 'sexy new Peugeot, hi-tech goodies, the ultimate family holiday in Disneyworld, a supermarket sprint, flowers and champagne and lots and lots of cash!' Lori Miles, one of those editors who seem to pop up whenever a new popular title is around (*Chat*, *Mizz*, etc.) was clear about her editorial mission. 'This is a magazine for you to enjoy; we're not here to change your life, turn you into some kind of superwoman, or find you a million things to do with an old horse blanket and a packet of dried egg!' (Whatever could she mean?) All the puzzles and competitions were wrapped round by cooking, horoscopes, a 'coffee break' short story, a vet's page, gardening and profiles. The formula has worked, and worked so well that *Take a Break* is now the biggest selling women's weekly magazine at 1.4 million. But *Take a Break*'s imitator from IPC not only did not work but failed lamentably. *Puzzle Weekly* came out in January 1992 with an initial print-run of 400,000. (By this time *Take a Break* had launched a spin-off called *Take a Puzzle*.) IPC cheekily billed their title the first women's weekly/puzzle magazine hybrid but maybe they had applied the blind eye to the telescope. The title nose-dived and IPC closed it a few months later, merging it into *Chat*.

National Magazines decided on an 'editorial refocus' of *She* magazine in February 1990, with an accent on older mothers – late starters in the baby stakes. They treated the refocus almost as a launch with trade and advertising presentations. Certainly *She* had been losing steam and its cheeky and disparate appeal. Linda Kelsey, editor of *Cosmopolitan* and herself an older mother, was given the task of changing the magazine to attract the new readership without, hopefully, losing too many of the older ones. There can be little doubt that the wide editorial changes have given the old trouper new life and circulation energy.

Condé Nast, publishers of *Vogue* and other glossies, threw a new sort of hat into the UK ring by launching *Vanity Fair*, the American magazine which had enjoyed startling success under the editorship of Tina Brown. It seemed tempting and logical to extend the publication of the title to this country but this would be different to any previous transatlantic movement of women's titles. *Vogue, Cosmopolitan, Good Housekeeping* and

House & Garden are examples of hugely successful American transplants, but the magazines published here are entirely different from their American parents. Indeed, the American roots are played down and ignored for the benefit of British readers. But *Vanity Fair* was to be the idential product on both sides of the Atlantic with only the advertising spaces being sold to British companies. This was a novel, and possibly hazardous, publishing tactic. As Oscar Wilde said, we have everything in common with the Americans except the language. As one of the advertising journals pointed out at the time of the *Vanity Fair* announcement, that month's American *Good Housekeeping* carried the cover line 'Twenty-eight days to thinner thighs and a firmer fanny', an aim capable of being misconstrued in this country. *Vanity Fair* was launched with modest circulation ambitions of 50,000. Nicholas Coleridge, now managing director of Condé Nast, said that *Vanity Fair* would be 'more than a coffee-table book for the very, very sophisticated. It has got glamorous and gritty coverage of news stories and is most like *Time* and *Newsweek*'.

This was perhaps an unfortunate comparison because it is the refusal of these two American news magazines to Anglicize their editorial that has kept their circulations so low in Britain with none of the essential-reading factor they enjoy in the States. *Vanity Fair* may appear to be a unisex magazine but Condé Nast market it as a women's magazine to the advertisers and seventy-five per cent of its readership is female.

Sex was definitely on the agenda in 1992. The upfront younger magazines like *Company*, *Cosmopolitan*, *More!* and *New Woman* had certainly not ignored the primeval urge. (As *More!* said on the back cover of their cover-mounted book on men: 'I'm in a job interview, scoring points with my intellect. Then, just as she's about to say "You've got the job" it occurs to me that she looks like Michelle Pfeiffer. My penis awakes from its quiet slumber and rears up to its full height.') *Company*, in particular, led the way down the garden path with overt sex articles and supplements that called a spade a spade – or a fork a fork. *Penthouse*, the top-shelf girlie magazine, full of wish-fulfilling, masturbatory massive-bosomed nudes, is now published by Northern & Shell. It seemed strategic to them that if the 1990s was the sex decade for women that was exactly what they would produce: a magazine called *For Women*. The magazine was sufficiently explicit to go up on the top shelf at the newsagents. The readers they sought were 'bold, intelligent, tough, cool and horny'. There would be plenty of naked young men and plenty of dangling genitalia. 'The success of recent sex supplements with more conventional women's magazines convinces us that the time is now right to launch *For Women*. Our aim is to push back the boundaries of women's magazines.' The editor, Jonathan Richards, saw that the age of the readers was unimportant. 'It is their attitude. Bold, upfront with sex. I think it will be quite liberating for women going into W.H. Smith's and reaching up to that top shelf.' The text of *For Women* is as open as the pictures, with oral sex, date rape and sex aids. Nothing is barred. Other titles have been added to the genre including *Women on Top* and the short-lived *Bite* from Ann Summers. *Bite* had no genitalia on display but otherwise held no inhibitions; sex was their thing and you got it in spades from fellatio to condom testing. *Bite* survived for less than one year.

In contrast, an old friend died in 1993 when D.C. Thomson closed *Jackie*, their 1963 magazine for teenage girls. The title *Jackie* was said to have been inspired by Mrs Kennedy, which would suggest a slightly more mature approach to the teen years than *Bunty* or *Mandy*. The first issue, 'for go-ahead teens', featured Cliff Richard on the front cover, gave away a twin-heart ring, offered super full colour pin-ups of Cliff, Elvis, Billy Fury and the Beatles, gave perfume tips 'for a more kissable you' and – their speciality – dreamy picture love stories. And twenty-nine years later the picture stories and the problem pages were still there but the circulation had been quite smashed by the likes of *Just Seventeen*, *More! Big!* and the music magazines. Poor old *Jackie* was obsolete and out of date, a symbol of a more naïve and less raucous age. 'Had the magazine's name not been so closely bound up with the late 1960s it could have persisted into the 1990s,' said Thomson. 'If the magazine had been called "Kylie" it might have lasted a bit longer. The title itself had become a bit outdated. We got to the stage where girls were finding their mums had read *Jackie* – and that really puts them off.'

The new titles continue to tumble out or to shuffle off the stage. The homes market goes bubbling on, the latest entrant to the *House Beautiful* arena being *Homemaker*. The BBC have taken the Antiques Road Show on to the newsstands with *Home & Antiques*, RAP Publishing contributed *Here's How*, a do-it-yourself title later renamed *HomeStyle*, and GE Publishing went for the crafts market with *Inspirations*. A pathetic attempt at a sort of female *Private Eye*, mixed with a touch of *Viz*, came with *Bitch* but a few issues saw it off. D.C. Thomson, as if to balance the loss of *Jackie*, launched *Shout*, 'the teenage magazine that's something to shout about!' (There had to be an explanation for that title. But D.C. Thomson have often been addicted to arcane one-word titles: *Catch*, *Etcetera* etc). Galaxy went for romance with *Affairs of the Heart* (the new magazine for women who like romance between the covers) and Fotopoli delivered *Fascination*, dealing with 'the other side of attractiveness'. *Spare Rib* went in 1993, after twenty years of waving the feminist flag, and *City Limits*, once a rival to *Time Out*, was ambitiously relaunched by Terry Hornett as a women's weekly targeting eighteen- to twenty-five-year-old women with a mixture of *More!* and *Time Out*. The experiment was unsuccessful, probably having caused confusion to some of its male gay readers. The swift demise was no surprise to pundits who could not visualize a London weekly for women, with or without the old association.

Health and fitness have always been subjects dear to women's magazines. Sometimes beauty is part of the editorial package but the whole gamut of slimming, exercise and medical advice is meat and drink to the editors. Health is a fickle subject upon which to base a magazine, with lots of comings and goings and usually about a dozen titles on the market with the word 'Health' in their logo. And the slimming magazines press on, though circulations are quite anorexic compared with the good old days. But the three survivors *Slimming*, *Slimmer* and *Weight Watchers* manage to clock up nearly half a million sales between them, even though none is a monthly. *Slimmer* puts out six issues a year, *Slimming* ten and *Weight Watchers* eight. EMAP had closed *Successful Slimming* after purchasing it as part of the job lot from Argus, and IPC faded out *Practical Health* in 1992. But two new entrants stepped on to the health stage in 1993, *BBC Good Health* and the ambitious *Top Santé* from Presse Publishing.

Top Santé is an Anglicized version of a popular French title which owes a lot of its success to television link-ups. The editor, Frankie McGowan, was the launch editor of *New Woman*. *Top Santé* was launched with a generous £1.5 million television campaign and branded itself as a mass-market women's magazine 'covering all aspects of health and beauty, well-being, psychology, sexuality, fitness and diet. *Top Santé* will meet the real needs of today's women every month'. The launch print-run of 400,000 was met with sales of 300,000 for the first few issues. The first front cover line of *BBC Good Health* ('for you and your family') led with the ambiguous announcement 'Making Good Sex Last'. They also offered to 'Shape That Bottom'. What promised to be an interesting duel between the BBC and the French unfortunately came to naught when the BBC withdrew their magazine, muttering darkly and sulking because they could not compete with the television spend of *Top Santé*. This was a bit rich coming from an organization that had obliterated magazine opposition with a drenching of free television plugs until that practice was stopped. As they explained: 'There is no way we could match *Top Santé* pound for pound in the market.' This was not a sign of healthy confidence.

Hello! seemed to have reached its zenith of circulation by early 1993 with sales a staggering 455,000. Competition and emulation were inevitable and Northern & Shell (of *Penthouse* and *For Women*) could not resist trying to get a chunk of this lucrative market. They brought out *OK!* (yet another obligatory exclamation) as a £1.95 monthly in April 1993. What was on offer? 'You'll visit the stars at home, share their tastes in food, fashion and leisure-time activities, catch up with the royals and step out with society.... Each month we'll feature competitions, with top prizes, book, film and theatre reviews, travel, horoscopes, puzzles....' And the first one-hundred-and-forty-eight-page issue boasted a glossy parade of the famous from the royal children to Jackie Collins, by way of Esther Rantzen, Ruby Wax and Jenny Agutter. There was a survey of the thirty most outstanding people in the world. *OK!* was setting itself up as posi-tive competition to *Hello!* But competition to neither was yet another exclamatory title. *Guess Who!* came from the *Daily Mail* company, Harmsworth Magazines. This was a buffoon of an attempt to nip in between *Hello!* and *Take a Break* by publishing lots of puzzles, crosswords, word games and quizzes featuring famous faces. You even had the opportunity to guess the identity of 'a top female celebrity' by the contents of her hand-bag. The answer, without peeking, had to be Joanna Lumley: it always is. (On second thoughts, it could have been Jilly Cooper.) *Guess Who!* had no chance and the *Daily Mail* shot it within a couple of months.

It was inevitable that Sainsbury's would want to get into magazines again. (Their *Family* in the 1960s was sold out to make *Family Circle*.) Tesco had discovered that magazines were a useful seller and stocked over two hundred titles but Sainsbury's were less convinced and took a few years to really get behind magazines as a commodity sell. When they eventually did, their next step was to move into 'own brand' and *Sainsbury's The Magazine* was launched in May 1993. A first-rate glossy production with the very competitive cover price of ninety-five pence, the magazine has the stamp of quality, concerning itself with many things non-Sainsbury. Consumerism, health, the arts, finance, Jilly Cooper (of course) relation-ships, travel, plus food, complete with some Delia Smith. It reads like a good general monthly magazine, but, of course, is overtly sales propa-ganda for the supermarket and its suppliers. At the low cover price, with the quality of the editorial, the magazine just cannot go wrong. The stores are saturated with copies when the new issue appears, an apparent sell-out each month. Copies sit in special racks at the entrance, at every check-out and in strategically placed gondolas. And each issue has special offer coupons for the stores. No wonder Thomson got out of the supermarket game!

There is nothing new about store-related magazines, sometimes paid for, sometimes free. Harrods and Selfridges both had their own eponymous titles, sold on the bookstalls as well as account customer distribution, but later abandoned them. Still going strong are the *M & S Magazine*, *Good Idea!* from Woolworths, *Your Choice* by the Co-op, *Hi-Time* for ASDA, *For You* given to customers of Forbuoys the newsagents, and estate agent titles from Foxtons and Savills.

Ageism is a concept that women's magazine publishers have been slow, or reluctant, to exploit. The so-called 'grey market' has its obvious economic attractions to the advertiser. The affluent couple with their mortgage paid up, education finished, the empty nest, the secure pension and lifetime savings. A time to enjoy leisure and to be able to spend money on oneself, travel, indulge. This dream scenario of the middle class would suggest a range of titles rushing on to the publishing stage but reality is different. Apart from three direct retirement magazines (*Choice* and *Yours* from EMAP and *Saga*) the national women's publisher has not seen the scope for magazines for older, or mature, women. The drawing boards have been busy in countless publishing offices, the computers have pumped out the statistics, the marketing men have been articulate, the editors have produced the dummies. But none of the big publishing houses have accepted the concept of an 'over forty' women's magazine. The reasons are disparate: a principal objection is that no woman wants to ask for a magazine that will brand her as old or mature. Would she move from her favourite magazine which covers her particular interests (food, fashion, gardening, etc.) to a title in which the common denominator is age? And what could such a magazine be named? All those euphemisms the Americans love, like 'golden age' or 'best of times', are too twee for this country. A hugely successful American magazine is *Modern Maturity* (which sounds like an insurance company), but this is a unisex title like *Saga*. Even America has not produced a women's magazine for the older market. The nearest to success was *Lear's*, produced for women over fifty or, as they put it, 'a magazine for the woman who wasn't born yesterday'. The same slogan was used for a new British magazine called

Chic, a title which in itself avoids any reference to the subject of age.

Chic is published by Hamerville and edited by Joyce Hopkirk, of *Cosmopolitan*, *Elle* and *She*. 'The idea for a new magazine', said Joyce, 'came from friends. They are among the seven million or so forty-somethings who, for one reason or another, want to do something new and positive with their lives.... I like the idea of writing for my own kind, grown-up women who don't fall apart when the first wrinkle appears.' Although there are the mandatory features on HRT, skin creams, and Jilly Cooper, a key section of the magazine is called 'Fresh Start' and emphasizes taking up new interests and learning new skills. Entertaining, cooking, travel, shopping, motoring, the arts and finance make up the rest of the editorial mix. *Chic* might be a breakthrough for grey journalism but the title is misleading and the cover strapline 'The Lifestyle Magazine for Women who can Choose' is a bit ambiguous. But as the population greys this is a magazine that might well flourish with the right editorial formula, given sufficient advertising and publisher investment.

As we plod our way towards the millenium, we can see that the state of the art of women's magazine publishing is more competitive, more volatile, more paranoid than ever. Women's magazines are big business, reaping rich rewards if the publisher gets it right or alarming losses if a new launch misses the target and pops its clogs. The business is now basically a game for the big boys, with EMAP, Condé Nast, IPC, National Magazines, Grühner & Jahr, Bauer and D.C. Thomson leading the pack. There are, of course, dozens of lesser companies with successful magazines, but it is the giant companies with the power of investment and experience who dominate the market and the future. Whether this diminution of separate publishing companies, compared to the 1950s, is a good thing is debatable but publishing major magazines is not for the cautious or lily-livered. Faint heart never wins fair readers these days. Big investment, big ideas and courageous launches are the industry's needs for the future. This is not to say that a small entrepreneur with a big idea cannot launch a new title and flourish; it just gets more hazardous as the years progress.

As we have seen in our whirlwind tour of history, the world has changed so much and the ambitions, expectations and power of women have moved forward so determinedly that magazine ideas and development have to be almost jet-propelled to keep up. Feminism has been the watchword in varying degrees of most of the younger magazines but the real issue has been independence. Women are now significant buyers of mortgages, investments, cars and travel. One fifth of all families are single parent, usually the mother. Magazines have been quick to reflect the changes of lifestyle of the independent woman.

Sex has become a predominant topic in most of the younger magazines. It has to be said that they have taken it to their bosoms with an over-abundance of enthusiasm. They analyse it, proselytize it, describe it, illustrate it, dissect it, romanticize it and generally wallow in it. No sexual holds have been barred, no byway unexplored. Sexual language is now explicit and words once seen only in textbooks or books with sealed covers sold in Soho, are now bandied freely about. This sexual freedom is not to be totally deplored, even if some magazines use it as a cynical camouflage for building circulation by shouting rude words in public. Sexual explicitness has spread downward from the *Cosmopolitan*s and *Company*s of the business, with their comparatively mature readerships, to the ever-younger teenage titles whose readers must by now be sexually aware and educated to a degree which would have baffled and perplexed previous generations. The exploration of sexual mores and sex education is to be applauded – it is the obsessive overuse of the subject as a continual one-upwomanship that gets tedious. Sex in magazines, as in all the other media, is here to stay but as the novelty of being explicit wears off it will probably get less attention from the editors.

Sex, of course, is not the sole preoccupation of women's magazines. It certainly buoys up circulation and delivers readers to the sales department. But the 1980s saw a shift back to some of the old basic magazine values so that the home titles flourished and the new 'practicals' did well. *Prima* and *Essentials* helped the swing back along, and *House Beautiful*, followed by a string of imitators, substantially added to the total readership of 'house' magazines. And the weekly market, once viewed by doom-laden pundits as being not too far from death's door, had a considerable kick forward by the German entries *Bella*, *Best* and *Take a Break*. All the IPC weeklies survived the Teutonic invasion even if their circulations were a bit shell-shocked. *Hello!* carved itself a surprise niche and rural life was hurtled into the women's market with the sturdy success of *Country Living* and *Country Homes*. The BBC cornered a new and profitable market sector with their string of programme-related titles, particularly food and gardening, and *Marie Claire* (not untinged with sex) proved that a good features magazine will find a ready audience.

Competition between magazines will be as intense as ever but a new element has crept in. Newspapers, particularly the tabloids, are increasingly becoming magazines, not only in their day-to-day features but with their Saturday and Sunday supplements, where the editorial is often directed towards women. The women's weeklies are vulnerable to this movement; as news is now predominantly in the fast-moving electronic media this trend will not go away. Newspapers move at the speed of Paul Revere compared to the box and the radio so the newspapers will increase their features element and become more like magazines.

I am always being told that there are too many women's magazines. A glance at the metres of shelves devoted to them in W.H. Smith or Tesco would seem to confirm this. There are about eighty magazines directly aimed at women but half the female population never read a women's magazine. My criticism, or unease, is not the number of magazines but the duplication. Too many titles are devoid of originality or innovation. The women's weeklies are particularly prone to this; a swap of front-cover logos would surely baffle the readers when most of the covers feature the royals, soap stars or pop idols. The monthlies also often follow the leader in style and content. The future has to lie with innovation, not parrot publishing. Going round the mulberry bush is not the way to create exciting new magazines. We need big editors with big ideas. *Hello!*, *House Beautiful*, *Marie Claire* and *Country Living* were mould breakers which have led, not followed. American publishers have created superstars like Helen Gurley Brown and the imported Tina Brown. It will be superstars who bring the market powerful new magazines, not just good editorial technicians.

The distribution of magazines will continue to cause resentment and rivalry. The supermarkets discovered magazines a few years ago and have taken them to their hearts with enthusiasm, both at the check-outs and in special sections. Publishers have found postal subscriptions are very effective in building and keeping sales, particularly for the quality monthlies. Newsagents, not unreasonably, resent both these methods of distribution; the copies on their shelves often contain advertising for cheaper postal subscriptions encouraging buyers to get their copies for less than sold by the newsagents. But women like receiving their magazines by post, and often the subscription copies carry special subscriber offers and treats. But most newsagents and multiples just get on with the job of selling millions of magazines. Publishers need the newstrade like a duck needs water. No launch could possibly take off without the newsagents.

So the publishing parade will go on marching past. We will see deaths of old friends and sudden flops of new aspirants. Some of the classics will continue to flourish, retuning themselves to the times. Some brilliant innovations will come out of the publishing woodwork, discovering new directions and ideas.

Women's magazines will continue to experience triumphs and disasters, even if they don't always treat those impostors just the same. As long as women want to read magazines, the publishers and editors will be only too ready to pander to their real and perceived desires. Sometimes they may even lead the readers and all of us to pastures new.

Appendices

I: WHO OWNS WHAT?

Here is a list of the bigger magazine houses and their women's titles. EMAP and IPC have divisions for their titles (Metro, Elan, Southbank etc.) but for simplification all the magazines are listed under the main company.

ARGUS	*Love Story*
	True Romances
	True Story
BAUER	*Bella*
	Take a Break
	Take a Puzzle
BBC MAGAZINES	*BBC Good Food*
	BBC Homes & Antiques
	Clothes Show Magazine
	BBC Vegetarian Good Food
CONDÉ NAST	*Vanity Fair*
	Vogue
	House & Garden
	World of Interiors
	Tatler
	Brides & Setting Up Home
EMAP	*Elle*
	Just Seventeen
	Looks
	More!
	Mother & Baby
	New Woman

	Parents
	Elle Decoration
	Period Living
	Big!
	Smash Hits
	Slimming
GRÜHNER & JAHR	*Best*
	Prima
IPC MAGAZINES LTD	*Chat*
	Essentials
	Family Circle
	Living
	Marie Claire
	Me
	Mizz
	19
	Options
	Woman
	Woman & Home
	Woman's Journal
	Woman's Own
	Woman's Realm
	Woman's Weekly
	Country Homes & Interiors
	Homes & Gardens
	Ideal Home
	Homes & Ideas
	MG
	My Guy Monthly
	Loving Magazine
	Practical Parenting
	Hair
NATIONAL MAGAZINE CO. LTD	*Company*
	Cosmopolitan
	Country Living
	Good Housekeeping
	Harpers & Queen
	House Beautiful
	She
REDWOOD	*M & S Magazine*
	Good Idea!

II: MERGERS

The following appendix shows some existing titles with their mergers over the years. Sometimes the merged titles had other titles put into them along the way but to simplify matters, I have given the dates of the deaths of the merged magazines.

EXISTING TITLE	MERGED TITLES
Family Circle	*Trio* (1964)
	Family (1964)
Good Housekeeping	*House Beautiful* (1968)
Harpers & Queen	*Queen* (1970)
	Harpers Bazaar (1970)
Ideal Home	*Housewife* (1968)
	In Store (1987)
19	*Woman & Beauty* (1963)
	Vanity Fair (1972)
	Honey (1986)
	Look Now (1988)
MG (*My Guy*)	*Petticoat* (1975)
	Boyfriend (1976)
	Intro (1976)
	Trend (1976)
	Hi! (1976)
	OK (1977)
	Fab (1980) *Fab Hits Fab 208*
	Pink (1980)
	Oh Boy! (1980)
	Mates (1981)
	Girl (1990)
My Guy Monthly	*Girl Monthly* (1989)
	Photo Loving Monthly (1990)
Woman	*Woman's Illustrated* (1961)
	Woman's Mirror (1966)
	ex *Woman's Sunday Mirror*
Woman & Home	*Modern Home* (1951)
	Modern Woman (1965)
	Everywoman (1967)
	My Home & Family (1971)
	Good Life (1980)

Woman's Journal	*Fashion* (1969)
	Flair (1972)
Woman's Own	*Woman's Life* (1934)
	Home Notes (1957)
	Woman's Day (1961)
Woman's Weekly	*Betty's Weekly* (1916)
	Woman's Companion (1961)
Loving Magazine	*True Monthly* (1989)
Homes & Gardens	*Weldon's Ladies Journal* (1954)
	Home Magazine (1963)
My Weekly	*Weekly Welcome* (1960)
	Secrets (1991)
Weekly News	*Celebrity* (1988)
Chat	*Puzzle Weekly* (1992)
Hair	*Hair & Good Looks* (1989)
Period Living	*Traditional Homes* (1992)

III: BIRTHS, MARRIAGES AND DEATHS

This is a listing of the main women's magazines that have been born, closed, or merged since the Second World War. The list includes the flops as well as successes and all the titles that are still alive at the time of writing. Frequency of publication is shown after the title, mainly F (fortnightly), M (monthly), W (weekly), Q (quarterly), or as noted.

Affairs of the Heart (M)
> Owners   Galaxy
> Launched   1991
> Died   1991

A La Carte (M)
> Owners   IPC Magazines Ltd
> Launched   1984
> Died   1989

Annabel (M)
> Owners   D.C. Thomson & Co. Ltd
> Launched   1966
> Died   1994

BBC Good Food (M)
    Owners BBC Magazines
    Launched 1989

BBC Good Health (M)
    Owners BBC Magazines
    Launched 1992
    Died (suspended) 1993

BBC Vegetarian Good Food (M)
    Owners BBC Magazines
    Launched 1992

Beauty & Skincare (twice per year)
    Owners Beauty & Skincare Publishing
    Launched 1980
    Died 1980

Bella (W)
    Owners Bauer (UK)
    Launched 1987

Best (W)
    Owners Grühner & Jahr (UK)
    Launched 1987

Big! (F)
    Owners EMAP Metro
    Launched 1990

Bitch (M)
    Owners Bitch Publications Ltd
    Launched 1992
    Died 1993

Bite (M)
    Owners Ann Summers Ltd
    Launched 1993
    Died 1994

Black Beauty & Hair (5 issues per year)
    Owners Hawker Consumer Publications Ltd
    Launched 1985

Blue Jeans (W)
>   Owners   D.C. Thomson & Co. Ltd
>   Launched   1987
>   Died   1991 (into *Jackie*)

Boyfriend (W)
>   Owners   City Magazines
>   Launched   1959
>   Died   1966 (into *Trend*)

Brides & Setting Up Home (alternate months)
>   Owners   Condé Nast Publications Ltd
>   Launched   1955

Britannia & Eve (M)
>   Owners   Illustrated Newspaper Group
>   Launched   1929 (absorbing *Eve*, launched 1919)
>   Died   1957

Cachet (M)
>   Owners   Cachet Ltd
>   Launched   1985
>   Died   1986

Candida (W)
>   Owners   IPC Magazines Ltd
>   Launched   1972
>   Died   1972

Capital Girl (W)
>   Owners   Gemini Publishing Ltd
>   Launched   1978
>   Died   1978

Catch (W)
>   Owners   D.C. Thomson & Co. Ltd
>   Launched   1989

Celebrity (W)
>   Owners   D.C. Thomson & Co. Ltd
>   Launched   1986
>   Died   1988 (into *Weekly News*)

Chat (W)
>Owners   (1) Publishing Developments Ltd
>(2) IPC Magazines Ltd
>Launched   1985

Chic (alternate months)
>Owners   Hamerville Magazines
>Launched   1993

Chic (M)
>Owners   Ratepress Ltd
>Launched   1984
>Died   1988

Clothes Show Magazine (M)
>Owners   (1) Focus
>(2) BBC Magazines
>Launched   1988

Company (M)
>Owners   National Magazine Co. Ltd
>Launched   1978

Cooks' Weekly (W)
>Owners   GH press Ltd
>Launched   1984
>Died   1988

Cosmopolitan (M)
>Owners   National Magazine Co. Ltd
>Launched   1972

Country Homes & Interiors (M)
>Owners   IPC Magazines Ltd
>Launched   1986

Country Living (M)
>Owners   National Magazine Co. Ltd
>Launched   1985

Date (W)
>Owners   Odhams Press
>Launched   1960
>Died   1961

Diana (W)
> Owners D.C. Thomson & Co. Ltd
> Launched 1964
> Died 1976 (into *Jackie*)

Elle (M)
> Owners (1) News International Hachette Ltd
>   (2) Hachette EMAP Consumer
> Launched 1985

Elle Decoration (alternate months)
> Owners Hachette EMAP Ltd
> Launched 1989

Essentials (M)
> Owners IPC Magazines Ltd
> Launched 1988

Etcetera (F)
> Owners D.C. Thomson & Co. Ltd
> Launched 1985
> Died 1986

Eve (W)
> Owners Morgan Grampian Ltd
> Launched 1973
> Died 1973

Everywoman (M)
> Owners Everywoman Ltd
> Launched 1986

Everywoman (M)
> Owners (1) Odhams
>   (2) IPC Magazines Ltd
> Launched 1934
> Died 1967

Exchange Contracts (twice per year)
> Owners H.H.L. Publishing
> Launched 1979

Executive Woman (Q)
> Owners Saleworld Publishing Ltd
> Launched 1987

Extra Special (alternate months)
    Owners (1) Extra Special
             (2) Maxwell Magazines
    Launched 1986
    Died 1988

Fab Hits (W)
    Owners IPC Magazines Ltd
    Launched 1964 (as *Fab*), incorporating *Boyfriend* (1966), *Intro* (1976), *Trend* (1976), *Hi!* (1976), *OK* (1977) *Petticoat* (1975)
    Died 1980 (into *Oh Boy!*)

Faces (W)
    Owners Marshall Cavendish
    Launched 1978
    Died 1978

Family (Q)
    Owners J. Sainsbury Ltd
    Launched 1961
    Died 1964 (into *Family Circle*)

Family Circle (M)
    Owners (1) International Thomson Publishing Ltd
             (2) IPC Magazines Ltd
    Launched 1964

Fashion (M)
    Owners Fleetway
    Launched 1968
    Died 1969 (into *Flair*)

Fashioncraft (alternate months)
    Owners Paterson Publications
    Launched 1981
    Died 1984

Fashion Folio (Q)
    Owners IPC Magazines Ltd
    Launched 1987
    Died 1988 (into *Marie Claire*)

Fiz (Q)
>   Owners   Home & Law Magazines
>   Launched   1982
>   Died   1985

Flair (M)
>   Owners   (1) Newnes
>   (2) IPC Magazines Ltd
>   Launched   1960
>   Died   1972 (into *Woman's Journal*)

Food Magazine (M)
>   Owners   (1) Perry Publications
>   (2) Trust House Forte
>   Launched   1979
>   Died   1984

For Women (M)
>   Owners   Northern & Shell PLC
>   Launched   1992

Freezer Family (M)
>   Owners   Freezer Family Ltd
>   Launched   1972
>   Died   1979 (into *Food Magazine*)

Girl (W)
>   Owners   IPC Magazines Ltd
>   Launched   1986
>   Died   1990 (into *My Guy*)

Girl Monthly (M)
>   Owners   IPC Magazines Ltd
>   Launched   1986
>   Died   1988 (into *My Guy Monthly*)

Girl About Town (W)
>   Owners   Girl about Town Ltd
>   Launched   1970

Glamour (W)
>   Owners   Amalgamated Press
>   Launched   1938
>   Died   1956 (merged into *Mirabelle*)

Good Housekeeping (M)
 Owners   National Magazine Co. Ltd
 Launched   1922

Good Idea! (3 times per year)
 Owners   Redwood Publishing (for Woolworths)
 Launched   1992

Good Life (M)
 Owners   IPC Magazines Ltd
 Launched   1978
 Died   1980 (into *Woman & Home*)

Guess Who? (M)
 Owners   Harmsworth Magazines
 Launched   1993
 Died   1993

Hair (alternate months)
 Owners   IPC Magazines Ltd
 Launched   1977

Hair & Beauty (Q)
 Owners   Reed Business Publishing
 Launched   1977
 Died   1990

Hair & Good Looks (alternate months)
 Owners   IPC Magazines Ltd
 Launched   1984
 Died   1989 (into *Hair*)

Hair Flair (M)
 Owners   Shaws Publications
 Launched   1982

Harper's Bazaar (M)
 Owners   National Magazine Co. Ltd
 Launched   1929
 Died   1970 (into *Harpers & Queen*)

Harpers & Queen (M)
 Owners   National Magazine Co. Ltd
 Launched   1970

Hello! (W)
    Owners Hello! Ltd
    Launched 1988

Here's How (M) (renamed *HomeStyle*)
    Owners RAP Publishing
    Launched 1992

Hers (M)
    Owners IPC Magazines Ltd
    Launched 1966
    Died 1984

Hi! (W)
    Owners IPC Magazines Ltd
    Launched 1975
    Died 1976 (into *OK*)

Hi-Time (alternate months)
    Owners ASDA
    Launched 1986

Home Chat (W)
    Owners Amalgamated Press
    Launched 1895
    Died 1958

Home Companion (W)
    Owners George Newnes
    Launched 1897
    Died 1956

Home Cooking (previously *Home & Freezer*) (M)
    Owners Argus Consumer
    Launched 1972 (as *Home & Freezer Digest*)

Home and Country (M)
    Owners National Federation of Women's Institutes
    Launched 1919

Home & Family (M)
    Owners The Mothers' Union
    Launched 1988

Home Flair (10 issues per year)
    Owners Hamerville Magazines
    Launched 1990

Home & Freezer Monthly (M)
>   Owners   (1) BEAP
>   (2) Seymour International
>   (3) House Press Manor
>   (4) Argus Consumer Publishing
>   Launched   1975 (as *Digest*)
>   Died   1991

Home Notes (W)
>   Owners   George Newnes
>   Launched   1894
>   Died   1957 (into *Woman's Own*)

Homes & Antiques (M)
>   Owners   BBC Magazines
>   Launched   1993

Homes and Gardens (M)
>   Owners   (1) George Newnes
>   (2) IPC Magazines Ltd
>   Launched   1919

Homes & Ideas (M)
>   Owners   IPC Magazines Ltd
>   Launched   1993

Honey (M)
>   Owners   (1) Fleetway
>   (2) IPC Magazines Ltd
>   Launched   1960
>   Died   1986 (into *19*)

House Beautiful (M)
>   Owners   National Magazine Co. Ltd
>   Launched   1989

House Beautiful (M)
>   Owners   National Magazine Co. Ltd
>   Launched   1954
>   Died   1968 (into *Good Housekeeping*)

House & Garden (M)
>   Owners   Condé Nast Publications Ltd
>   Launched   1947

Housewife (M)
    Owners 1. Hulton Press
               2. Odhams Press
    Launched 1939
    Died 1967 (into *Ideal Home*)

Ideal Home (M)
    Owners (1) Odhams Press
              (2) IPC Magazines Ltd
    Launched 1920

Inhabit (M)
    Owners Link House
    Launched 1973
    Died 1974

Inspirations (M)
    Owners G.E. Publishing Ltd
    Launched 1993

In Store (M)
    Owners IPC Magazines Ltd
    Launched 1985
    Died 1987 (into *Ideal Home*)

Intro (W)
    Owners Odhams Press Ltd
    Launched 1967
    Died 1967

Jackie (W)
    Owners D.C. Thomson & Co. Ltd
    Launched 1963
    Died 1993

Just Seventeen (W)
    Owners EMAP Metro Publications Ltd
    Launched 1983

Kitchen Choice (M)
    Owners Oberon Publishing
    Launched 1984
    Died 1985

The Lady (W)
Owners   The Lady
Launched   1885

Let's Cook! (M)
Owners   Grühner & Jahr (UK)
Launched   1990
Died   1991

Living (M)
Owners   (1) International Thomson Publishing Ltd
         (2) IPC Magazines Ltd
Launched   1967

Looking Good (M)
Owners   Penny Vincenzi Publications Ltd
Launched   1972
Died   1973

Look Now (M)
Owners   (1) Carlton Magazines
         (2) IPC Magazines Ltd
Launched   1972
Died   1988 (into *19*)

Looks (M)
Owners   EMAP Metro Publications Ltd
Launched   1985

Love Affair (W)
Owners   IPC Magazines Ltd
Launched   1970
Died   1982 (into *Loving*)

Loving Magazine (M)
Owners   IPC Magazines Ltd
Launched   1970

M & M (Maternity & Mothercraft) (alternate months)
Owners   H.H.L. Publishing
Launched   1967

M & S Magazine (Q)
Owners   Redwood Publishing
Launched   1987

Marie Claire (M)
   Owners   European Magazines Ltd
   Launched   1988

Marilyn (W)
   Owners   Amalgamated Press
   Launched   1957
   Died   1965

Marty (W)
   Owners   George Newnes
   Launched   1959
   Died   1963

Mates (W)
   Owners   IPC Magazines Ltd
   Launched   1975
   Died   1981 (into *Oh Boy!*)

Mayfair (M)
   Owners   Spry Publications Ltd
   Launched   1946
   Died   1950

Me (W)
   Owners   IPC Magazines Ltd
   Launched   1989

Metropolitan Home (M)
   Owners   Harmsworth Magazines (and Meredith USA)
   Launched   1990
   Died   1991

Mirabella (M)
   Owners   Murdoch Magazines
   Launched   1990
   Died   1991

Mirabelle (M)
   Owners   (1) Amalgamated Press Ltd
             (2) IPC Magazines Ltd
   Launched   1956
   Died   1977 (merged into *Pink*)

Mizz (F)
> Owners   IPC Magazines Ltd
> Launched   1985

Ms London (W)
> Owners   Commuter Publishing Partnership
> Launched   1968

Modern Woman (M)
> Owners   George Newnes
> Launched   1925 (included *Modern Home* 1928–51)
> Died   1965

More! (M)
> Owners   EMAP Metro Magazines Ltd
> Launched   1988

Mother   (incorporating *Modern Mother*) (M)
> Owners   (1) IPC Magazines Ltd
>   (2) Argus
>   (3) EMAP Elan
> Launched   1936
> Died   1990

Mother & Baby (M)
> Owners   (1) Argus
>   (2) EMAP Elan
> Launched   1956

MG (My Guy) (W)
> Owners   IPC Magazines Ltd
> Launched   1978

My Home & Family (M)
> Owners   Fleetway
> Launched   Contained *My Home* (1928) and *Wife & Home*
>   (1929)
> Died   1971 (into *Woman & Home*)

My Weekly (W)
> Owners   D.C. Thomson & Co. Ltd
> Launched   1910

New Homemaker (previously *Homemaker*) (M)
    Owners IPC Magazines Ltd
    Launched 1980 (*Homemaker* 1969)
    Died 1981 (into *Practical Householder*)

New Woman (M)
    Owners (1) Murdoch Magazines
            (2) Hachette/EMAP Magazines Ltd
    Launched 1988

19 (M)
    Owners IPC Magazines Ltd
    Launched 1968

Nova (M)
    Owners (1) George Newnes
            (2) IPC Magazines Ltd
    Launched 1965
    Died 1975

Office Secretary (Q)
    Owners Trade Media Ltd
    Launched 1987

Oh Boy! (W)
    Owners IPC Magazines Ltd
    Launched 1976
    Died 1985 (into *My Guy*)

OK (W)
    Owners IPC Magazines Ltd
    Launched 1975
    Died 1977 (into *Fab 208*)

OK! (F)
    Owners Northern & Shell PLC
    Launched 1933

Options (M)
    Owners (1) Carlton Magazines
            (2) IPC Magazines Ltd
    Launched 1982

Parents (M)
 Owners (1) Gemini Magazines
         (2) Argus
         (3) EMAP Elan
 Launched 1976

Patches (W)
 Owners D.C. Thomson & Co. Ltd
 Launched 1979
 Died 1989 (into *Blue Jeans*)

People's Friend (W)
 Owners D.C. Thomson & Co. Ltd
 Launched 1869

Perfect Home (M)
 Owners DMG Home Interest Magazines
 Launched 1992

Period Living & Traditional Homes (M)
 Owners EMAP Elan
 Launched 1990

Personal (M)
 Owners Carlton Magazines
 Launched 1974
 Died 1975

Petticoat (W)
 Owners Fleetway
 Launched 1966
 Died 1975 (into *Hi!*)

Pink (W)
 Owners IPC Magazines Ltd
 Launched 1973
 Died 1980 (into *Mates*)

Pins & Needles (M)
 Owners (1) International Thomson Publishing
         (2) Consumer & Industrial Press
 Launched 1949
 Died 1989

Practical Parenting (M)
>   Owners   (1) International Thomson Publishing Ltd
>   (2) IPC Magazines Ltd
>   Launched   1988

Pretty Big (Q)
>   Owners   Pretty Big Publishing
>   Launched   1993

Pride Magazine (alternate months)
>   Owners   The Voice Communications Group
>   Launched   1993

Prima (M)
>   Owners   BSR (Publishing) Ltd
>   Launched   1976
>   Died   1977

Prima (M)
>   Owners   Grühner & Jahr (UK)
>   Launched   1986

Puzzle Weekly (W)
>   Owners   IPC Magazines Ltd
>   Launched   1992
>   Died   1993 (into *Chat*)

Queen (F)
>   Owners   (1) Several
>   (2) Stevens Press 1957
>   (3) Oxley Press 1968
>   (4) National Magazine Co. Ltd
>   Launched   1861
>   Died   1970 (merged with *Harper's Bazaar* into *Harpers & Queen*)

Red Star Weekly (W)
>   Owners   D.C. Thomson & Co. Ltd
>   Launched   1929
>   Died   1983

Rio (M)
>   Owners   Link House
>   Launched   1981
>   Died   1982 (into IPC's *Hers*)

Riva (W)
>   Owners   Carlton Magazines
>   Launched   1988
>   Died   1988

Romany (M)
>   Owners   Petulengro Magazines
>   Launched   1983
>   Died   1985

Romeo (W)
>   Owners   D.C. Thomson & Co. Ltd
>   Launched   1957
>   Died   1974 (into *Diana*)

Roxy (W)
>   Owners   Amalgamated Press Ltd
>   Launched   1957
>   Died   1963

Sainsbury's The Magazine (M)
>   Owners   New Crane Publishing Ltd (for Sainsbury's)
>   Launched   1993

Secrets (W)
>   Owners   D.C. Thomson & Co. Ltd
>   Launched   1932
>   Died   1991 (into *My Weekly*)

She (M)
>   Owners   National Magazine Co. Ltd
>   Launched   1955

Sheba (M)
>   Owners   Sheba Publications Ltd
>   Launched   1979
>   Died   1980

Shout (F)
>   Owners   D.C. Thomson & Co. Ltd
>   Launched   1993

Sincerely (M)
>   Owners   (1) George Newnes
>   (2) IPC Magazines Ltd
>   Launched   1958
>   Died   1961 (into *True*)

Slimmer (alternate months)
Owners Turret Group PLC
Died 1975

Slimming (10 issues per year)
Owners (1) Slimming Magazine Ltd
(2) Argus
(3) EMAP Elan
Died 1969

Slimming Naturally (alternate months)
Owners Newman Turner Publications Ltd
Launched 1978
Died 1980

Spare Rib (M)
Owners Spare Rib Ltd
Launched 1972
Died 1993

Stitchcraft (M)
Owners Stitchcraft Ltd
Launched 1932
Died 1982

Successful Slimming (alternate months)
Owners (1) IPC Magazines Ltd
(2) Argus
(3) EMAP Plan
Launched 1976
Died 1990

Take a Break (W)
Owners H. Bauer
Launched 1990

Taste (M)
Owners (1) Marshall Cavendish
(2) BEAP
(3) Focus
(4) Al Fresco
(5) Taste Publishing Ltd
(6) H.H.L./Drew Smith
Launched 1986
Suspended 1994

Tatler (M)
> Owners (1) Various
> (2) Illustrated Newspapers
> (3) Thomson
> (4) County Illustrated Group
> (5) Tatler & Bystander Publishing
> (6) Condé Nast

Launched 1709 (died 1966, relaunched briefly as *London Life*, resurrected in 1968 as *Tatler*)

Tomorrow (alternate months)
> Owners Katherine Hamnett
> Launched 1985
> Died 1985

Top Santé (M)
> Owners Presse Publishing
> Launched 1993

The Townswoman (M)
> Owners National Union of Townswomen's Guilds
> Launched 1933

Traditional Homes (M)
> Owners (1) C.F.E. Publishing
> (2) Benn Consumer Periodicals Ltd
> (3) Burleigh Magazines
> (4) EMAP Elan

Launched 1984 (now into *Period Living*)

Trend (W)
> Owners City Magazines Ltd
> Launched 1966
> Died 1967 (into *Petticoat*)

True (M)
> Owners IPC Magazines Ltd
> Launched 1954
> Died 1984

True Monthly (M)
> Owners IPC Magazines Ltd
> Launched 1987
> Died 1990 (into *Loving Monthly*)

True Romances (M)
   Owners   Argus
   Launched   1934

True Story (M)
   Owners   Argus
   Launched   1922

Unison (10 issues per year)
   Owners   Landmark Publishing
   Launched   1993

Valentine (W)
   Owners   Fleetway
   Launched   1957
   Died   1974

Vanity Fair (M)
   Owners   (1) National Magazine Co. Ltd
            (2) IPC Magazines Ltd
   Launched   1949
   Died   1972 (merged into IPC's *Honey*)

Vanity Fair (M)
   Owners   Condé Nast Publications Ltd
   Launched   1991

Viva (M)
   Owners   Penthouse Publications
   Launched   1974
   Died   1979

Vogue (M)
   Owners   Condé Nast Publications Ltd
   Launched   1916

W (F)
   Owners   Queensway Publishing
   Launched   1987
   Died   1988

Wedding and Home (alternate months)
   Owners   (1) Socio Magazines
            (2) Home & Law
            (3) IPC Magazines Ltd
   Launched   1975

Weight Watchers (8 issues per year)
    Owners   (1) Weight Watchers
             (2) Harmsworth Magazines
    Launched 1977

Weldon's Ladies' Journal (W)
    Owners Amalgamated Press
    Launched 1875
    Died 1954 (into *Home*, which was merged into *Homes & Gardens* 1963)

Woman (W)
    Owners   (1) Odhams Press
             (2) IPC Magazines Ltd
    Launched 1937

Woman & Beauty (M)
    Owners George Newnes
    Launched 1930
    Died 1963

Woman, Bride and Home (alternative months)
    Owners   (1) Odhams Press
             (2) IPC Magazines Ltd
    Launched 1968
    Died 1972

Womancraft (M)
    Owners   (1) Astra Press
             (2) National Magazine Co. Ltd
             (3) IPC Magazines Ltd
             (4) Paterson Publications
    Launched 1972
    Died 1982 (into *Sewing & Knitting*)

Woman and Home (M)
    Owners   (1) Amalgamated Press (Fleetway)
             (2) IPC Magazines Ltd
    Launched 1926

Woman's Companion (W)
    Owners Amalgamated Press
    Launched 1927
    Died 1961 (into *Woman's Weekly*)

Woman's Day (W)
    Owners George Newnes
    Launched 1958
    Died 1961 (into *Woman's Own*)

Woman's Friend (W)
    Owners Pearsons (Newnes)
    Launched 1924
    Died 1950 (into *Glamour*)

Woman's Illustrated (W)
    Owners Odhams Press
    Launched 1936
    Died 1961 (into *Woman*)

Woman's Journal (M)
    Owners (1) Amalgamated Press (Fleetway)
           (2) IPC Magazines Ltd
    Launched 1927

Woman's Mirror (W)
    Owners (1) Fleetway
           (2) IPC Magazines Ltd
    Launched 1958 (formerly *Woman's Sunday Mirror* 1955)
    Died 1966 (into *Woman*)

Woman's Own (W)
    Owners (1) George Newnes
           (2) IPC Magazines Ltd
    Launched 1932

Woman's Pictorial (W)
    Owners Amalgamated Press
    Launched 1920
    Died 1956 (into *Home Chat*)

Woman's Realm (W)
    Owners IPC Magazines Ltd
    Launched 1958

Woman's Weekly (W)
    Owners IPC Magazines Ltd
    Launched 1911

Woman's World (M)
Owners   Carlton Magazines Ltd
Launched   1977
Died   1990

Woman's World (W)
Owners   Odhams Press
Launched   1903
Died   1958

Working Woman (M)
Owners   Wintour Publications
Launched   1984
Died   1987

World of Interiors (M)
Owners   Condé Nast Publications Ltd
Launched   1981

Index